DOING THE WORKS OF JESUS

DOING THE WORKS OF JESUS

BOOK 1

BECOMING A DISCIPLE WHO LOVES

ALAN DRAKE

SPIRIT OF WISDOM PUBLICATIONS

DALLAS, TEXAS

ISBN-10: 0989850900
ISBN-13: 978-0989850902
Library of Congress Control Number: 2013920010

Printed in the United States of America

To my parents

Zane and Shirley Drake

CONTENTS

INTRODUCTION
WHAT IS THIS ALL ABOUT?

This is about learning practical ways to demonstrate the power and love of Jesus Christ to people we encounter every day.

This is about bringing the reality of Christ into our daily lives.

This is about living a life of power and love on a daily basis.

This is about learning to walk in the Spirit moment by moment.

This is about fully becoming the person God intends for you to be and living the abundant life that God intends for you to live.

This is about all of us becoming a Church that demonstrates the reality of Christ to a dying world that needs to see proof!

This is about learning to do the works of Jesus (John 14:12).

> Whoever says he abides in him ought to walk in the same way in which he walked.—1 John 2:6 (ESV)

CHAPTER 1
THE NEXT STEP

Ministry Is for All Believers

Maybe you are like me. I am not employed in "full-time Christian ministry." I don't run a nonprofit organization. I have worked in secular jobs for more than twenty-five years. At the present time, I have no official ministry title. I do not hold a staff position at my local church, but I am a minister of Jesus Christ.

For the last few years, I have felt driven to understand and obtain the promise contained in John 14:12. In that passage, Jesus makes this amazing statement: "Most assuredly, I say to you, he who believes in Me, the works that I do he will do also; and greater works than these he will do, because I go to My Father" (NKJV). Jesus didn't present this as merely a possibility. This is a *promise*! If a believer meets the condition of faith, Jesus promises that believer that he *will* do the works of Jesus, and greater works than these he *will* do!

This promise is not only for church leaders. It is for *all* believers. Jesus didn't single out church leaders when He made this promise. In fact, there were no religious leaders in the room when He said this! Your church leaders may or may not ever experience the full potential of this promise, but don't let that stop you! You don't need to wait on your church leaders before you take the challenge and begin "doing the works of Jesus." If this desire is in your heart like it is in mine, *go for it!* Remember that when the time came for Jesus to choose his twelve apostles, who would be entrusted to carry on His ministry after He was gone, Jesus did not choose religious leaders. He bypassed the "Bible schools" of the time and chose ordinary people and prepared them to do extraordinary things.

It's important for us to remember that the pastor was never meant to do all of the work of the ministry. In Ephesians 4:12 (AMP), Paul tells us that when Jesus gave apostles, prophets, evangelists, pastors, and teachers to the Church, "His intention was the perfecting and the full equipping of the saints (His consecrated people), [that they should do] the work of ministering..."

The Church is described as the Body of Christ, with many members. We all have unique, essential functions to perform. Each of us has a vital role to fulfill.

In His letters to the seven churches in Revelation chapters 2 and 3, Jesus first gave specific messages to the entire church membership; but at the end of each message, He gave a special invitation that promised amazing reward, not to the whole church, but to the individual who set himself or herself apart from the rest and accepted His challenge to be an overcomer. In those messages, Jesus seems to imply that He knows that not every church member will take the challenge. He addresses only those individuals who desire more, those who are not satisfied with the ordinary, and those who are willing to make any sacrifice to overcome and obtain the extraordinary ultimate prize.

Will you take the challenge that Jesus is offering? Will you leave the ordinary behind, choosing instead to overcome whatever obstacles might stand in your way and obtain the extraordinary prize, doing the works of Jesus, and even greater works?

What Should I Hope to Get out of This?

The goal here is *not* to prepare you to fill a position on the church organizational chart. The goal is to help empower you to fulfill the desire that God has already put into your heart for ministry.

You have a calling of God on your life. One of the goals of this book is to help prepare you to discover and fulfill the purpose that God has for your life and to learn more about who you really are in Christ.

This book offers practical tools that can help empower you to do the works of Jesus, as He promised that we would (John 14:12), and to fulfill Christ's command to love one another, as He has loved us (John 15:12).

As each one of us becomes a disciple who really loves Jesus and really loves people—and demonstrates that on a daily basis—the Church will be transformed. We will become a Church that truly is a light to the city, to the nation, and to the world.

As we learn to focus on giving to the needs of others, rather than on just getting blessings for ourselves, our lives will demonstrate true Christianity to others, and we will be taking the first steps toward fulfilling Christ's "Great Commission" to go and make disciples of all the nations, teaching them to observe everything that Jesus commanded us (Matthew 28:19–20).

CHAPTER 2
THE CHALLENGE

The Cares of This Life

You may have a deep desire to serve God in ministry, but other needs may seem to be taking priority. How can you get involved in ministry to others when you have so many needs yourself?

Do you need to be healed?

Do you have serious financial needs?

Do you have problems that are tearing your family apart?

Do you have a very difficult situation at your job?

Are things missing from your life?

God's Response:

He invites you to cast your cares on Him, for He cares for you (1 Peter 5:7).

It is natural to seek first to meet our own needs and the needs of our family members, but God invites us to make an exchange. He invites us to cast our concerns on Him, and He promises to care for us better than we could take care of ourselves. In exchange, He desires for us to take on His concerns, His priorities, and seek to meet the needs of His Kingdom first. This is the message contained in Matthew 6:25–34.

> People who are ungodly run after all of those things. Your Father who is in heaven knows that you need them. But put God's kingdom first. Do what he wants you to do. Then all of those things will also be given to you. So don't worry about tomorrow. Tomorrow will worry about itself. Each day has enough trouble of its own.—Matthew 6:32–34 (NIRV)

In the first chapter of Haggai, God exhorts us not to neglect the needs of His house. We may think that we must give priority to meeting our own needs and taking care of our own houses—our own families. In truth, the harder we work at meeting our own needs and desires, and those of our families, the further behind we often get. If we truly consider our situations, we are inadequate to provide for our own needs and desires and those of our families.

God never equipped us to do that. It was never His plan for us to be self-sufficient. If we will take Him up on His offer to exchange our cares for His, He will take care of us and our families better than we ever could!

> The Lord who rules over all says, "The people of Judah are saying, 'The time hasn't come yet for the Lord's temple to be rebuilt.'"

So the message came to me from the Lord. He said, "My temple is still destroyed. In spite of that, you are living in your houses that have beautiful wooden walls."

The Lord who rules over all says, "Think carefully about how you are living. You have planted many seeds. But the crops you have gathered are small. So you eat. But you never have enough. You drink. But you are never full. You put your clothes on. But you are not warm. You earn your pay. But it will not buy everything you need."

He continues, "Think carefully about how you are living. Go up into the mountains. Bring logs down. Use them to rebuild my house. Then I will enjoy it. And you will honor me," says the Lord.

"You expected a lot. But you can see what a small amount it turned out to be," announces the Lord who rules over all. "I blew away what you brought home. Why? Because my temple is still destroyed. In spite of that, each one of you is busy with your own house.

"So because of what you have done, the heavens have held back the dew. And the earth has not produced its crops. I ordered the rain not to fall on the fields and mountains. Then the ground did not produce any grain. There were not enough grapes to make fresh wine. The trees did not bear enough olives to make oil. People and cattle suffered. All of your hard work failed."—Haggai 1:2–11 (NIRV)

It is the divine order for the servant to serve the master *first*. It is only *after* the master is satisfied that the servant sits down to have his needs satisfied.

"Which of you, having a slave plowing or tending sheep, will say to him when he has come in from the field, 'Come immediately and sit down to eat'? But will he not say to him, 'Prepare something for me to eat, and properly clothe yourself and serve me while I eat and drink; and afterward you may eat and drink'?"—Luke 17:7–8 (NASB)

This was the divine order that Jesus observed.

Meanwhile the disciples were urging Him, saying, "Rabbi, eat." But He said to them, "I have food to eat that you do not know about." So the disciples were saying to one another, "No one brought Him anything to eat, did he?"

Jesus said to them, "My food is to do the will of Him who sent Me and to accomplish His work.—John 4:31–34 (NASB)

When Jesus was in the wilderness, the enemy tempted him to give in and satisfy his own needs prematurely (Matthew 4:3), but Jesus refused. A great victory for the Kingdom of God was at stake. After Satan's temptations were overcome and the victory was won, Jesus not only ate, but He was served by angels! God personally took care of Him (Matthew 4:11).

If you will trust God with your personal needs and seek His Kingdom first, He will honor that by providing what you need in return. God invites you to make an exchange. If you take care of His Kingdom, His Church, His Family, He will personally take care of you, your house, and your family in return.

Aligned with Kingdom Purposes

In July 2009, I was on my way to minister in Scotland. I arrived in Edinburgh on my second day of travel. Because of flight changes, my luggage did not arrive in Edinburgh when I did. The problem was that I was about to catch a bus to St Andrews, fifty miles away, and I would not be back in Edinburgh for a week. As I spoke with the airline agent, he took my lodging information and assured me that my bag would be delivered to me after it arrived. So I thanked him, got on the next bus to St Andrews, and I was off.

I arrived in St Andrews a couple of hours later, checked into my room, and walked down the road to the conference that I had come to attend. When I went back to my room that night, my bag had still not arrived. The next day, I attended the morning sessions of the conference wearing the same clothes for the third day.

Meanwhile my friends offered to drive me to stores to buy clothes and toiletries. I turned them down because I didn't want them to miss part of the conference to take me shopping, but I was more concerned now.

I stopped to pray.

It had not been necessary for me to have my bag until now, but the next day, I would begin ministering to the children in the morning and to the adults in the afternoon. In my prayer, I stated my case to God by saying that if I did not get my bag that day, His Kingdom work would suffer. I would be forced to minister to the children with a three-day beard, bad breath (because I didn't have toothpaste), and smelly, dirty clothes. I made my case that some of the children would not respond to me in that condition, and they might even be afraid of me.

After lunch I went back to the residence hall where I was staying and asked at the front desk whether my bag had arrived. The lady behind the desk replied, "Yes, Mr. Drake. Your bag is waiting for you in your room."

In my prayer, when I made my case that the Kingdom work was at stake, there were immediate results. You could say that this was a coincidence of timing, but I've noticed that as I seek God's Kingdom first and trust Him to take care of meeting my needs, these "coincidences" happen more consistently.

My God Shall Supply All Your Need

In 1981, I was attending classes at the University of Texas at Arlington. On the morning of my final exam in statistics, I made plans to stop by a poor widow's house and leave some money with her before I went on to class. She was experiencing difficult financial circumstances, so I put some money in an envelope and labeled it "from Jesus." I drove to her house, stuck it in her screen door, and drove on to the university, which was about thirty minutes away.

After I parked my car and began walking across campus to my class, I realized to my horror that I had forgotten my calculator!

In this particular statistics class every problem involved adding up large columns of numbers and then performing various calculations on the sums of those large numbers. Without a calculator, I would be forced to add up all of those numbers by hand, which would take much more time. I was hit with the realization that I would never be able to finish the test in the allotted time.

After all of the time and effort I had put into this class, it now seemed inevitable that I would fail the final exam and possibly fail the class!

As I thought through my options, I knew there would not be enough time for me to drive back home to get my calculator. None of the stores was open this early in the morning, so I couldn't buy a new calculator. I didn't know anyone who lived in the area who might be able to bring me a calculator. There seemed to be no options available to me. I walked to the testing room, resigned to the realization that I would probably fail the exam.

I was one of the last students to enter the testing room. The test-takers were all sitting at large round tables. Few empty seats were left. As I took a seat at a table, I looked to my left, and was surprised to see that the student on my left had brought an extra calculator! We were not friends, but she let me use her extra calculator. I finished the test before she did, handed the calculator back to her, and went on my way. I made an A in the class.

Why would anyone bring an extra calculator to take a test?

I'm convinced that because I took steps to seek first the Kingdom of God and to help provide for the needs of this widow, God made sure that my needs were provided for.

> Here are the kinds of beliefs that God our Father accepts as pure and without fault. When widows and children who have no parents are in trouble, take care of them. And keep yourselves from being polluted by the world.—James 1:27 (NIRV)

The Desires of Our Hearts

One day a brochure came in the mail to my office. The brochure was about a training conference in Boston. Immediately I was struck with a longing to travel.

On the cover of the brochure was a photo of the sculpture in the Boston Common of the ducklings depicted in Robert McCloskey's book *Make Way for Ducklings*. I know exactly where that sculpture is. If you dropped me into the city of Boston, I could walk directly to it. This photo immediately brought back good memories of traveling to Boston and other cities and spending days just seeing as much as I could possibly take in while I was there. Years ago that had been one of my favorite things to do.

The memories triggered by the brochure photo brought back a desire to travel—to get away, take a trip for two or three days, and just spend time enjoying exploring another city.

As I thought it over, I decided against it. My conscious decision was "No, my money needs to go into the Kingdom now." But I kept the brochure because the picture brought back fond memories of traveling.

The next morning, first thing, my phone rang. It was the secretary in another department whose son worked for Southwest Airlines. She told me that he had a ticket that he was not going to use, and she wondered if I would like to use it. She didn't know anyone else who would use it, and it would expire if it was not used within the next several days. She told me that it was good for any Southwest Airlines destination.

I told her that I would be thrilled to take it, and then she asked me what my choice of destination might be. She did some checking online and created possible weekend travel itineraries for Boston, Chicago, and Washington, DC.

I settled on Chicago because I had never really spent much time there, and she took care of all of the arrangements for the ticket. She also told me that, because it was a company voucher, I would be flying standby, so she advised me not to check any luggage, but to take everything in a carry-on bag. That presented a small problem because I didn't have a carry-on bag that would be able to hold a weekend's worth of stuff.

After work that day, after all the flight arrangements had been made, I stopped by my brother's house to see how their garage sale was going. Just before I left, I spotted something under a table that caught my eye.

My cousin, who is a pilot for Northwest Airlines, had donated two of his older carry-on bags to my brother's garage sale. One of them was perfect for what I needed for my trip to Chicago! I would never have bought a brand-new bag for just one weekend trip, but this one was perfect, and it cost next to nothing! I gave my sister-in-law some money for the bag, and in less than a day, I was all set for a weekend trip to Chicago. I got online later and booked a hotel to complete the preparations for the trip. Lodging, food, and a parking charge at the airport were my only expenses.

I thoroughly enjoyed my time in Chicago. I would not have gone had the plane ticket not been provided for me, but I believe the Lord saw the desire of my heart, and in this case, when I made a conscious choice to put the Kingdom work ahead of my own desires, God granted those desires.

Delight yourself in the Lord; And He will give you the desires of your heart.—Psalm 37:4 (NASB)

Test Him

"Bring the whole tithe into the storehouse, so that there may be food in My house, and test Me now in this," says the LORD of hosts, "if I will not open for you the windows of heaven and pour out for you a blessing until it overflows. Then I will rebuke the devourer for you, so that it will not destroy the fruits of the ground; nor will your vine in the field cast its grapes," says the LORD of hosts.—Malachi 3:10–12 (NASB)

In this passage from Malachi, God invites us to test Him with the tithe and allow Him to prove that He is faithful to bless us abundantly in return.

If you have taken God up on this challenge and have proven Him to be faithful to bless you when you tithe, why not trust Him in this as well? Why not give Him a chance to prove that

He will be faithful to take care of *all* your needs when you focus on seeking His Kingdom first?

You Will "Discover" Your True Life

Then Jesus said to His disciples, If anyone desires to be My disciple, let him deny himself [disregard, lose sight of, and forget himself and his own interests] and take up his cross and follow Me [cleave steadfastly to Me, conform wholly to My example in living and, if need be, in dying, also].

For whoever is bent on saving his [temporal] life [his comfort and security here] shall lose it [eternal life]; and whoever loses his life [his comfort and security here] for My sake shall find it [life everlasting].

For what will it profit a man if he gains the whole world and forfeits his life [his blessed life in the kingdom of God]? Or what would a man give as an exchange for his [blessed] life [in the kingdom of God]?

For the Son of Man is going to come in the glory (majesty, splendor) of His Father with His angels, and then He will render account and reward every man in accordance with what he has done.—Matthew 16:24–27 (AMP)

"But *Other* People Aren't Doing What *They're* Supposed to Do!"

This is absolutely true, but wouldn't it be a tragedy if you allow this to be your excuse for losing out on all that God has for *you*? Instead of looking to the people who are making poor life choices, we can find encouragement in the lives of others like the Apostle Paul who have forsaken all else to pursue God's best. We can take courage in the examples of those who have simplified their lives to a single focus of "forgetting what lies behind and straining forward to what lies ahead, I press on toward the goal to win the [supreme and heavenly] prize to which God in Christ Jesus is calling us upward."—Philippians 3:13–14 (AMP).

"But What If I Don't Feel Qualified?"

Join the club! Here are a few of God's champions who have been members of that group:

- Moses (Exodus 3:11)

- Gideon (Judges 6:15)

- David (1 Samuel 16:11)

- Jeremiah (Jeremiah 1:6)

- Peter (Luke 5:8)

- Insert your name alongside other great champions of God!

> But He said to me, My grace (My favor and loving-kindness and mercy) is enough for you [sufficient against any danger and enables you to bear the trouble manfully]; for My strength and power are made perfect (fulfilled and completed) and show themselves most effective in [your] weakness. Therefore, I will all the more gladly glory in my weaknesses and infirmities, that the strength and power of Christ (the Messiah) may rest (yes, may pitch a tent over and dwell) upon me!—2 Corinthians 12:9 (AMP)

Consider the example of Elisha (2 Kings 13:20–21). He died and was entombed. Talk about unqualified for future ministry! You can't get any more "unqualified" than dead! You would think that ministry would be over for him at that point, but wait!

A dead man was lowered into Elisha's tomb. As soon as the dead man's body touched the bones of Elisha, the man revived and stood on his feet!

Elisha didn't even allow the fact that he was physically dead to stop him from ministering to others! Even though he could not raise himself from the dead, he didn't let that stop him from raising another man! Now, what's your excuse?

(Bible scholars will have all kinds of problems with my application of Elisha's story. I'll let them worry about that. My purpose here is to encourage you to step into doing the works of Jesus, even if you feel unqualified.

There are those who spend their entire lives only *studying* the Word of God, and then there are those who *become* a living, breathing word of God, reaching out to demonstrate the love and power of God to the people they encounter.

My prayer is that you will join the second group.)

You yourselves are our letter. You are written on our hearts. Everyone knows you and reads you. You make it clear that you are a letter from Christ. You are the result of our work for God. You are a letter written not with ink but with the Spirit of the living God. You are a letter written not on tablets made out of stone but on human hearts.—2 Corinthians 3:2–3 (NIRV).

CHAPTER 3
STEP INTO MATURITY

So...Where Should We Start?

Where should we start? What should we look to as our model for ministry? I believe it can be found in John 14:12 (NKJV):

> Most assuredly, I say to you, he who believes in Me, the works that I do he will do also...

In fact, that is *just a starting point* for us. The promise of Jesus is that we will start there, and then we will go on to experience even "greater works." Let's look at the ministry of Jesus as a place to start.

Jesus' Helpmate

Doesn't that make sense? If we are destined to be the bride of Christ, shouldn't we begin to act as the "helpmate" that our Lord needs by His side, joining with Him in His work? It would be a tragedy for us to squander the time we have here and come to the end of our journeys only to be told by the Lord that we are strangers to Him. Unfortunately, that will be the reality for some.

> ...the bridegroom came, and those who were prepared went in with him to the marriage feast; and the door was shut. Later the other virgins also came and said, Lord, Lord, open [the door] to us! But He replied, I solemnly declare to you, I do not know you [I am not acquainted with you].—Matthew 25:10–12 (AMP)

What Does It Look Like to Do the Works of Jesus?

Let's look at an overview of the three stages of growth in the Christian life. This will give us an overall picture of the goals of each of the three stages. Then we will have a clearer picture of the ultimate goals of mature Christian ministry.

Faith	Hope	Love

3 Stages of the Christian Life

Salvation and Survival	Receiving God's Blessing and Power	Meeting the Needs of Others

"The greatest of these is love."—1 Cor. 13:13

The first stage is characterized primarily by faith. We are saved by grace through faith (Ephesians 2:8). When we first become born again, we are spiritually very much like physical newborns. We are vulnerable and very needy, but we have no idea what we need or how to get our spiritual needs met. Peter addresses this when he says, "as newborn babes, desire the pure milk of the word, that you may grow thereby"—1 Peter 2:2 (NKJV). We are dependent on God and mature Christian leaders to help protect us, nourish us and guide our growth.

The second stage of maturity is characterized by hope. We don't leave faith behind. We build on faith and grow in hope, learning to believe God's promises and gaining courage as we are being prepared to fulfill our future destiny.

> For I know the plans I have for you, declares the Lord, plans for welfare and not for evil, to give you a future and a hope.—Jeremiah 29:11 (ESV)

The final stage of maturity is characterized by love. The first two stages of growth involve getting, getting, and more getting on the part of the believer. Getting our needs met. Getting blessings. Getting power. Getting training. Getting correction. The third stage turns the focus completely around. It is all about giving—giving to meet the needs of others. Getting doesn't stop, but that is overshadowed now by the higher focus of giving. The third stage is much like being a parent. In fact, that is how John describes this third stage of maturity. When he speaks to believers at this stage of maturity, he addresses them as fathers.

> I am writing to you, fathers, because you have come to know (recognize, be aware of, and understand) Him Who [has existed] from the beginning. I am writing to you, young men, because you have been victorious over the wicked

[one]. I write to you, boys (lads), because you have come to know (recognize and be aware) of the Father.—(1 John 2:12–14).

Of course, there is neither male nor female in Christ (Galatians 3:28), so the masculine terms that John uses here speak of a spiritual truth, rather than a physical truth. *Spiritual* young men and *spiritual* fathers can be males or females *physically*.

Faith	Hope	Love

3 Stages of the Christian Life
1 John 2:12–14

Little Boys	Young Men	Fathers
		1 Cor. 4:15
		Mal. 4:6

"The greatest of these is love."—1 Cor. 13:13

As John indicates, the little boys have just become aware of God. They have just begun to recognize Him. They have received salvation by grace through faith and have just begun their spiritual lives.

Young men have grown beyond the childhood stage. They are growing stronger, becoming mighty in spirit (Ephesians 3:16). They are learning much as they submit to spiritual authorities and teachers (Galatians 4:1–2). They are experiencing some success in overcoming sin and evil (Luke 10:17).

But God's goal for each of us is to become a mature spiritual father. *(Remember, there is neither male nor female in Christ.)* Fathers are no longer focused primarily on their own needs, their own interests, and their own agendas. They find their purpose and fulfillment in meeting the needs of others. Job was such a man. God praised Job very highly, saying that there was no one like him in the whole world. And how did Job describe himself?

> I was a father to the poor and needy; the cause of him I did not know I searched out.—Job 29:16 (AMP)

These three stages of maturity are identifiable in Abraham's life as he grew from a life characterized by faith, to one of hope, waiting on the fulfillment of God's promise, to the life of a father, characterized by love and giving.

Faith	Hope	Love

3 Stages in Abraham's Life

Believing God's Promise	Seeking Fulfillment of the Promise	Giving the Promised Son Back to God

"The greatest of these is love."—1 Cor. 13:13

But the greatest example of these three stages of growth can be seen in the life of Jesus, our ultimate model. He was born to be our Messiah, the Savior of all mankind. Simeon and Anna recognized this when Jesus was just a baby in the temple (Luke 2:21–38). It took Jesus thirty years of preparation to grow to maturity until He was finally ready to fulfill this calling on His life. During that time, He submitted Himself to His parents (Luke 2:51), learned obedience (Hebrews 5:8), and grew stronger (Luke 2:40). In the fullness of His maturity, He dedicated His life to serving others, meeting their needs, and giving His life so that others might find Life.

Faith	Hope	Love

3 Stages in Jesus' Life

Born with incredible promises to fulfill	He grew strong in spirit, increased in wisdom and stature, and in favor with God and man. Luke 2:40, 52	"...the Son of Man did not come to be served, but to serve, and to give His life a ransom for many." Mark 10:45

"The greatest of these is love."—1 Cor. 13:13

Very simply, *that* is what it means to "do the works of Jesus"—living a life focused on serving others, meeting their needs, and giving our lives so that they might find Life, "and that they might have it more abundantly" (John 10:10 KJV). God's goal in the life of every Believer is to bring us to that level of maturity. *You are ready* to hear this call to maturity, even if you may not feel that you are.

God is compelling you—drawing you—up to this level of maturity.

> Let each of you look out not only for his own interests, but also for the interests of others.—Philippians 2:4 (NKJV)

> Bear one another's burdens, and so fulfill the law of Christ.—Galatians 6:2 (NKJV)

> Are you willing?

CHAPTER 4
OUTSIDE THE CHURCH WALLS

As we begin to examine the ministry of Jesus, it is remarkable to realize that most of the significant events in Jesus' ministry happened outside of the "church" meetings of His day—meetings in the synagogues and meetings in the temple.

In contrast, for most Christians in our day, the focus of our spiritual activity centers on church meetings. Our spiritual lives often revolve around church meetings. These meetings are often our source of stability and spiritual grounding.

We may need to rethink that paradigm, because Jesus did not seem to center His ministry or His relationship with His Father, on "church" meetings. The most significant acts of His ministry took place outside of church meetings:

• Jesus was not "in church" when He called His disciples.

• Jesus' miracle ministry did not begin in a "church" meeting.

• Jesus healed many more people outside of "church" meetings than in "church" meetings.

• Jesus' greatest sermons and greatest miracles occurred outside of "church."

If the only recorded events in Jesus' ministry had been those that occurred in the "church" meetings of His day, there would be very few healings and miracles detailed in the Gospels. His ministry would look very different—and not very impressive, really, for the Son of God and the Savior of all mankind. Only when you look at what Jesus did *outside* of traditional "church" meetings do you see the real substance of His ministry, and you see the life we are also called to enter into.

Events in Jesus' Ministry

On the next few pages, I've listed the significant events in Jesus' ministry, putting them into two groups—those that occurred in the synagogues and in the temple and those events that happened outside of those traditional "church meetings" of that time. The list is not comprehensive or perfectly chronological, but the purpose of this list is to illustrate the fact that *the vast majority of significant events in Jesus' ministry happened outside of "church meetings."*

The setting is not clear in Scripture for some events, so those events may be listed in both columns and indicated by (?). During some of the feasts, for instance, events may or may not have occurred in a temple meeting.

Outside of "Church"	In "Church"
• Baptized by John—Mt 3, Mk 1, Lk 3	
• Temptation—Mt 4, Mk 1, Lk 4	
• Andrew believes—Jn 1	
• Jesus meets Peter—Jn 1	
• Jesus calls Philip—Jn 1	
• Nathanael believes—Jn 1	
• First miracle at Cana wedding—Jn 2	
	• Cleansed the temple—Jn 2
• Miracles at Passover (?)—Jn 2	• Miracles at Passover (?)—Jn 2
• Nicodemus visits Jesus—Jn 3	
• Disciples baptize in Judea—Jn 3	
• Woman at the well—Jn 4	
• Many Samaritans believe—Jn 4	
• Galileans welcome Jesus—Jn 4	
• Nobleman's son raised up—Jn 4	
	• Jesus teaches in the synagogues (Galilee)—Lk 4
	• Jesus reads from Isaiah 61 (Nazareth)—Lk 4
	• People try to kill Jesus—Lk 4
	• Jesus teaches in Capernaum—Mt 4, Mk 1, Lk 4
	• Evil spirit cast out—Mk 1, Lk 4

OUTSIDE OF "CHURCH"	IN "CHURCH"
• Peter's wife's mother healed—Mt 8, Mk 1, Lk 5	
• Devils cast out; many healed—Mt 8, Mk 1, Lk 4	
• Jesus goes to isolated place—Mk 1, Lk 4	
• People follow Jesus; try to make Him to stay—Mk 1, Lk 4	
	• Jesus preaches; casts out devils—Mk 1, Lk 4
• Jesus teaches from Peter's boat—Lk 5	
• Peter's great catch of fish— Lk 5	
• Peter, Andrew, James, John follow Jesus—Mt 4, Mk 1, Lk 5	
• Jesus cleanses a man's leprosy—Mt 8, Mk 1, Lk 5	
• Jesus' fame grows; multitudes follow Him; all kinds of sickness healed— Mt 4	• Jesus teaches in synagogues—Mt 4
	• Jesus preaches Gospel, healing all kinds of sickness (?)—Mt 4, Lk 5
• Jesus withdraws and prays—Lk 5	
• Jesus heals man lowered through roof—Mt 9, Mk 2, Lk 5	
• Jesus teaches by seaside— Mk 2	

OUTSIDE OF "CHURCH"	IN "CHURCH"
• Jesus calls Matthew—Mt 9, Mk 2, Lk 5 • Jesus eats with sinners—Mt 9, Mk 2, Lk 5 • Man at Bethesda pool healed—Jn 5 • Jesus' disciples pluck corn on the Sabbath—Mt 12, Mk 2, Lk 6	
	• Jesus teaches in synagogue; heals man with withered hand—Mt 12, Mk 3, Lk 6 • Pharisees plot to kill Jesus—Mt 12:14, Mk 3:6, Lk 6:11
• Jesus withdraws; heals all who come to Him—Mt 12, Mk 3 • Jesus heals blind, mute man—Mt 12, Lk 11 • Jesus accused of casting out devils by Beelzebub—Mt 12, Mk 3, Lk 11 • Jesus prophesies the sign of Jonah—Mt 12 • Jesus describes unclean spirits that are cast out—Mt 12 • Jesus goes to mountain; prays all night—Mk 3, Lk 6 • Jesus ordains 12 apostles—Mk 3; Lk 6 • Jesus comes to the plain; heals all who come to Him—Lk 6	

Outside of "Church"	In "Church"
• Sermon on the Mount—Mt 5–7, Lk 6	
• Centurion's servant healed—Mt 8, Lk 7	
• Young man raised from dead—Lk 7	
• John the Baptist questions Jesus—Mt 11, Lk 7	
• Jesus speaks to people about John the Baptist—Mt 11, Lk 7	
• Jesus pronounces woes on unrepentant cities—Mt 11	
• Jesus invites all who are weary to come to Him—Mt 11	
• Jesus goes with the twelve through every city and village preaching and showing the good news of the kingdom of God; healing every sickness and disease—Mt 9, Mk 6, Lk 8	• Jesus teaches in synagogues—Mt 9, Mk 6
• Jesus speaks in parables—Mt 13, Mk 4, Lk 8	
• Jesus declares His true mother and brothers—Mt 12, Mk 3, Lk 8	
	• Jesus teaches in synagogue at Nazareth, but cannot do many mighty works there—Mt 13, Mk 6

OUTSIDE OF "CHURCH"	IN "CHURCH"
• Jesus speaks about having nowhere to lay His head and to let the dead bury the dead—Mt 8	
• Jesus calms the storm—Mt 8, Mk 4, Lk 8	
• Gadarene man delivered of legion of demons—Mt 8, Mk 5, Lk 8	
• Jesus returns by ship; the people gladly receive him—Mk 5, Lk 8	
• Jairus' daughter raised from the dead—Mt 9, Mk 5, Lk 8	
• Woman with issue of blood healed touching the hem of Jesus' garment—Mt 9, Mk 5, Lk 8	
• Two blind men following Jesus are healed—Mt 9	
• Jesus gives twelve disciples power and authority over all devils and to cure diseases; sends them out to preach the Kingdom of God and to heal the sick—Mt 10, Mk 6, Lk 9	
• Jesus withdraws with apostles to desert place—Mt 14, Mk 6, Lk 9, Jn 6	
• Jesus speaks to people about the Kingdom, healing them that need healing—Mt 14, Mk 6, Lk 9, Jn 6	

Outside of "Church"	In "Church"
• Jesus feeds the five thousand—Mt 14, Mk 6, Lk 9, Jn 6	
• People want to make Jesus king; He sends disciples to other side of the lake; dismisses the crowds; goes up on a mountain to pray— Mt 14, Mk 6, Jn 6	
• Jesus walks on water—Mt 14, Mk 6, Jn 6	
• People come to Jesus in Gennesaret, bringing all who were sick; as many as touch His garment are healed; Jesus declares Himself the Bread of Life— Mt 14, Mk 6, Jn 6	
• Pharisees question Jesus about breaking traditions and not washing hands— Mt 15, Mk 7	
• Daughter of Syro-Phoenician woman healed—Mt 15, Mk 7	
• Great crowds bring many people needing healing; Jesus heals them—Mt 15, Mk 7, Jn 7	
• Jesus heals deaf man with speech impediment—Mk 7	
• Jesus feeds four thousand—Mt 15, Mk 8	

Outside of "Church"	In "Church"
• Jesus cautions disciples about leaven of Pharisees and Saducees—Mt 16, Mk 8	
• Jesus heals blind man at Bethsaida—Mk 8	
• Peter's confession of faith—Mt 16, Mk 8, Lk 9	
• Jesus foretells His suffering, rejection, death and resurrection—Mt 16, Mk 8, Lk 9	
• Peter rebukes Jesus—Mt 16, Mk 8	
• Jesus describes the cost and rewards of discipleship—Mt 16, Mk 8, Lk 9	
• Jesus' transfiguration—Mt 17, Mk 9, Lk 9	
• Jesus heals epileptic boy—Mt 17, Mk 9, Lk 9	
• Jesus again foretells being delivered into the hands of men—Mt 17, Mk 9, Lk 9	
• Jesus pays taxes out of fish's mouth in Capernaum—Matt 17	
• Jesus teaches that whoever is least is great, and that he who is not against us is for us—Mk 9, Lk 9	
	• Jesus goes to Feast of Tabernacles in Jerusalem—Jn 7

OUTSIDE OF "CHURCH"	IN "CHURCH"
	• Jesus teaches in the temple—Jn 7
	• Woman caught in adultery—Jn 8
	• Jesus speaks with Jews and Pharisees in the temple—Jn 8
	• Jews try to stone Jesus; Jesus leaves the temple—Jn 8
• Jesus heals man born blind; Jews cast the man out of the synagogue; he confesses belief in Jesus as Son of God—Jn 9	
• Jesus declares Himself the Good Shepherd—Jn 10	
	• Jesus attends the Feast of Dedication—Jn 10
	• Jesus declares that His works bear witness of Who He is; He and the Father are one—Jn 10
	• Jews again try to stone Jesus; then try to arrest Him—Jn 10
• Jesus crosses Jordan River; many believe in Jesus there—Jn 10	
• Jesus responds to conditions people place on following Him—Lk 9	

Outside of "Church"	In "Church"
• Jesus sends out the seventy-two to heal and declare the Kingdom of God—Lk 10	
• The seventy-two return with joy; they are given all power over the enemy; Jesus rejoices—Lk 10	
• Good Samaritan—Lk 10	
• Jesus & Mary & Martha— Lk 10	
• Jesus teaches on prayer— Lk 11	
• People accuse Jesus of casting out devils through the prince of devils; Jesus explains what happens when devils are cast out— Lk 11	
• Jesus responds to a woman who blesses the womb that bore Jesus and the breasts that fed Him—Lk 11	
• Jesus describes an evil generation that seeks a sign and the consequences—Lk 11	
• The light of a candle; the light of the body—Mk 4, Lk 11	
• Jesus dines with a Pharisee without washing His hands; declares woes on Pharisees and lawyers—Lk 11	

Outside of "Church"	In "Church"
• Jesus speaks to the innumerable multitude—Lk 12 • Man asks Jesus to speak to his brother to divide the inheritance—Lk 12 • Jesus teaches the parable of rich man; take no thought for your life; seek first the Kingdom; be ready for the Lord's return; He came not to bring peace, but division; discern the time; agree with your adversary lest he deliver you to the judge—Lk 12 • Except you repent, you shall all likewise perish—Lk 13 • Parable of the fruitless fig tree—Lk 13	
	• Jesus heals woman in the synagogue on the Sabbath who had been bowed over for eighteen years—Lk 13 • The Kingdom of God is like growing seed; a grain of mustard seed; like leaven hidden in meal—Mk 4, Lk 13
• Jesus goes through cities and villages, teaching and journeying toward Jerusalem—Lk 13	

Outside of "Church"	In "Church"
• Jesus declares many shall seek to enter in, but shall not be able—Lk 13	
• Pharisees warn Jesus to get out or Herod will kill Him—Lk 13	
• Jesus mourns over Jerusalem—Mt 23, Lk 13	
• Jesus heals man with dropsy and justifies healing on the Sabbath—Lk 14	
• Jesus advises taking the lowest seat at feasts and gatherings; inviting the poor to your dinners, not your friends; and shares the parable of the unworthy dinner invitees—Lk 14	
• The cost of discipleship—Lk 14	
• Salt that has lost its savor—Mk 9, Lk 14	
• Parables of the lost sheep; and the lost coin—Lk 15	
• The Prodigal Son—Lk 15	
• Parable of the unjust steward; he that is faithful in least is faithful in much; no man can serve two masters—Lk 16	
• The law and the prophets until John—Lk 16	
• Divorce, remarriage, adultery, and celibacy—Mt 19, Mk 10, Lk 16	

OUTSIDE OF "CHURCH"	IN "CHURCH"
• Rich man and Lazarus—Lk 16	
• Woe to the world because of offenses—Mt 18, Mk 9, Lk 17	
• Whoever is least is great; consequences for offending little ones—Mt 18, Mk 9, Lk 17	
• Parable of the Lost Sheep— Mt 18	
• Dealing with offenders—Mt 18, Lk 17	
• Parable of the Unforgiving Servant—Mt 18	
• Faith as mustard seed—Lk 17	
• Servant serves the master before he eats—Lk 17	
• Jesus departs from Galilee and comes to region of Judea beyond Jordan; great multitudes follow; He heals them there—Mt 19, Mk 10	
• Ten lepers healed—Lk 17	
• The Kingdom of God is within you—Lk 17	
• As in the days of Noah and Lot—Lk 17	
• Parable of the widow and the unjust judge—Lk 18	
• Parable of the Pharisees' and the publicans' prayers—Lk 18	

Outside of "Church"	In "Church"
• Suffer the little children to come—Mt 19, Mk 10, Lk 18	
• The rich, young ruler—Mt 19, Mk 10, Lk 18	
• Parable of the workers in the vineyard—Mt 20	
• Jesus foretells his suffering and death—Mt 20, Mk 10, Lk 18	
• Mother of James and John asks that her sons be seated beside Jesus in His kingdom—Mt 20, Mk 10	
• Jesus heals blind beggar(s) by side of road—Mt 20, Mk 10, Lk 18	
• Zacchaeus receives Jesus—Lk 19	
• Parable of the talents—Mt 25, Lk 19	
• Jesus hears that Lazarus is sick; raises him from the dead—Jn 11	
• Jews plot to kill Jesus; Jesus goes to Ephraim with the disciples—Jn 11	
• Jesus arrives near Bethphage and Bethany at the Mount of Olives—Mt 21, Mk 11, Lk 19, Jn 12	
• A dinner is held in Jesus' honor; Mary anoints the feet of Jesus, wiping them with her hair—Jn 12	

Outside of "Church"	In "Church"
• Large crowd comes to see Jesus and Lazarus; Chief priests plot to kill Lazarus—Jn 12 • Jesus sends two disciples to get a colt; Jesus rides to Jerusalem on the colt—Mt 21, Mk 11, Lk 19, Jn 12 • Jesus weeps over Jerusalem—Lk 19	
	• Jesus casts buyers and sellers out of the temple—Mt 21, Mk 11, Lk 19 • Jesus teaches daily; heals blind and lame in the temple; spends nights on Mount of Olives; early in the mornings all people come to the temple to hear Him—Mt 21, Mk 11, Lk 19, 21
• The fig tree withers—Mt 21, Mk 11	
	• Religious leaders question Jesus' authority—Mt 21, Mk 11, Lk 20 • Parable of two sons—Mt 21 • Parable of the wicked tenants—Mt 21, Mk 12, Lk 20 • The chief cornerstone—Mt 21, Mk 12, Lk 20 • Religious leaders try to find a way to arrest Jesus—Mt 21, Mk 12, Lk 20

Outside of "Church"	In "Church"
	• Parable of the wedding feast—Mt 22
	• Render to Caesar—Mt 22, Mk 12, Lk 20
	• Sadducees question the resurrection—Mt 22, Mk 12, Lk 20
	• The greatest commandment—Mt 22, Mk 12
	• How is Christ the son of David?—Mt 22, Mk 12, Lk 20
	• Beware of the scribes; woes to scribes and Pharisees—Mt 23, Mk 12, Lk 20
	• The widow's mites—Mk 12, Lk 21
	• Greeks seek Jesus—Jn 12
• Future events for Israel, the Church and the world—Mt 24, Mk 13, Lk 21	
• Parable of the ten virgins—Mt 25	
• Separation of sheep and goats—Mt 25	
• Jesus foretells His crucifixion at Passover to his disciples—Mt 26	
	• Judas plots with the chief priests and captains to betray Jesus—Mt 26, Mk 14, Lk 22

Outside of "Church"	In "Church"
• Jesus declares "The hour has come for the Son of Man to be glorified," and "Whoever believes in Me believes in Him Who sent me"—Jn 12	
• The Last Supper—Mt 26, Mk 14, Lk 22	
• Jesus washes the disciples' feet—Jn 13	
• Jesus declares His betrayer—Mt 26, Mk 14, Lk 22, Jn 13	
• Jesus answers the disciples' contention about which of them is greatest—Lk 22	
• Jesus gives a new commandment—Jn 13	
• Jesus prophesies the falling away of His disciples; Peter's betrayal; after He is risen, He will go before them into Galilee—Mt 26, Mk 14, Lk 22, Jn 13	
• Jesus' farewell talk to disciples—Jn 14–16	
• Jesus prays to His Father—Jn 17	
• Jesus tells disciples to take provisions and swords—Lk 22	
• Jesus and disciples sing a hymn—Mt 26, Mk 14	

OUTSIDE OF "CHURCH"	IN "CHURCH"
• Jesus prays in Gethsemane—Mt 26, Mk 14, Lk 22, Jn 18 • Jesus' betrayal and arrest; high priest's ear is cut off, Jesus heals him—Mt 26, Mk 14, Lk 22, Jn 18	
	• Jesus' trial (religious)—Mt 26, Mk 14, Lk 22, Jn 18 • Peter's denial—Mt 26:69, Mk 14:66, Lk 22:55, Jn 18:15
• Jesus' trial (legal)—Mt 27, Mk 15, Lk 23, Jn 18–19 • Jesus mocked by soldiers—Mt 27, Mk 15 • The road to Golgotha—Mt 27, Mk 15, Lk 23, Jn 19 • Jesus is crucified—Mt 27, Mk 15, Lk 23, Jn 19 • Jesus' body is placed in the tomb—Mt 27, Mk 15, Lk 23, Jn 19 • The empty tomb and risen Christ—Mt 28, Mk 16, Lk 24, Jn 20 • Jesus appears to the women—Mt 28, Mk 16, Jn 20 • Jesus meets two disciples on the road to Emmaus—Mk 16, Lk 24 • Jesus appears to the disciples in Jerusalem—Mk 16, Lk 24, Jn 20	

Outside of "Church"	In "Church"
• Jesus appears to the disciples by the Sea of Tiberius—Jn 21 • Jesus asks Peter three times if he loves Him; Peter asks Jesus about John—Jn 21 • Disciples meet Jesus in Galilee; Great Commission; instructions to wait in Jerusalem for the promise of the Father—Mt 28, Mk 16, Jn 20, Acts 1 • Jesus' ascension—Mk 16, Lk 24, Acts 1	

Could God be trying to tell us something here? If most of the significant events in Jesus' life and ministry occurred outside of "church meetings," the same will be true in our lives! His life is our model!

The "In-Between" Times

One thing that you may notice as you examine the list of significant events in Jesus' ministry is that very few of them were scheduled. For example,

• Jesus was only passing through Samaria when he met the woman at the well. Some might call this a "chance encounter," but it resulted in revival coming to the entire city of Sychar.

- A woman's son was raised from the dead in Luke 7 when he was carried out at the same time *as Jesus was walking by* the funeral party.

- The Gadarene man was delivered of the Legion of evil spirits after he met Jesus on the shore.

- Jairus' daughter was raised from the dead after her father begged Jesus to come to his house.

- *On the way to Jairus' house*, the woman with the issue of blood was healed when she touched the hem of Jesus' garment.

- Bartimaeus received his sight *when Jesus passed by* where he was sitting by the side of the road.

- Peter's confession came *as they were on their way* to the towns of Caesarea Philippi.

- Zacchaeus was saved after Jesus called to him *as He was passing by*.

- And so on, and so on...

In each of these situations, Jesus was *on his way to go somewhere else* when this "interruption" in His schedule happened.

What we begin to realize is that we may schedule events that we consider significant, but *God causes divine appointments to happen during the times* in-between *these scheduled events* that many times turn out to be the *real* significant events in our lives. We must recognize that God works in the "in-between" times.

In your heart you plan your life. But the Lord decides where your steps will take you.—Proverbs 16:9

Lord, I know that a man doesn't control his own life. He doesn't direct his own steps.—Jeremiah 10:23

The steps of a good man are ordered by the LORD, And He delights in his way.—Psalm 37:23

In March, 2005, I traveled to New Hampshire to attend a training class that would prepare me to teach a particular course. A group of believers had traveled from Scotland to attend that same class. As we visited with each other between sessions during this week-long class, I met Zach, Rick, and Heather. At one point, Zach, whose ministry was based in the UK, invited me to travel to St Andrews, Scotland, to participate with ministry teams that he directed during the CLAN Gathering Christian conference each summer. (CLAN is an acronym for "Christians Linked Across the Nation.") After attending my first CLAN, I was hooked, and I went back again to participate the following year.

But things changed after that, and Zach moved on to other things and was no longer leading those ministry teams. At that point, I figured that my time there might be over because the teams might be turned over to someone who didn't know me. However, the teams were turned over to Rick, who already knew me and who invited me to continue ministering with those teams the next year. After another year or two, team leadership again changed hands as Rick moved on to bigger responsibilities. This time, team leadership was entrusted to Heather, whom I had also met in the New Hampshire training class, and I continued to be invited back to help with this team of ministers.

Ironically, I no longer teach the course that I traveled to New Hampshire to be trained for, but as of this writing, I am planning my seventh trip to Scotland to minister with my friends at CLAN Gathering.

So...what was God's real purpose for the New Hampshire training class? In my mind, I was scheduling a time to be trained to teach a particular course. But God had other plans. In between sessions during that week of training, He arranged for me to connect with people who would open doors for me to minister in Scotland—doors that I could never have opened myself, no matter how much planning I did!

It was my attendance at the CLAN Gathering conferences that really brought this principle home to me, that God arranges appointments for us in between our scheduled events.

During the CLAN Gathering conferences, I attended many sessions taught by wonderful leaders. At the beginning of each session, I would start a new page in my notebook, writing the title of the session at the top of the page. But more than once, at the end of the session, I would look down at a blank piece of paper. I had written nothing in my notebook. But I would walk out of the session and have significant, memorable, encounters with people who I ended up writing about in my notebook at the end of the day.

It happened so often that the stark contrast was undeniable. At the end of the week, as I looked back, flipping through notes I had taken over the course of the week, the most significant events were the unplanned, unscheduled encounters I had with people in between the scheduled sessions.

Jesus' life was like that. Most of the significant events in His ministry occurred in between scheduled events, as He was going from place to place. They were "interruptions" in His schedule. Our lives are like that, too. We just need to wake up to that fact.

This is God's way—to work in between our scheduled events. As another example, God instructs us to use these "in-between" times wisely to teach His commandments to our children.

> You shall teach them diligently to your children, and shall talk of them when you sit in your house, when you walk by the way, when you lie down, and when you rise up.— Deuteronomy 6:7 and 11:19 (NKJV)

Here, He specifically directs us to make use of times when we are sitting at home, when we are walking around, when we are lying down, and when we are rising up. He is purposely describing those times when we are in between scheduled events—when we may have returned from one event and have some time before preparing for another event in our schedule.

Seeing Interruptions from God's Point of View

Divine appointments come disguised as interruptions. They come with bad attitudes, at inconvenient times, acting inappropriately. Examples include the Gaderene demoniac, the Syrophonecian woman, blind men crying out by the side of the road...almost every significant encounter Jesus had.

Jesus didn't demand that people clean themselves up and approach him with respectful, appropriate attitudes, using proper protocol before He reached out to minister to them in love. He met them as they were when they crossed His path and touched them with the love and power of God to meet their needs.

But God demonstrates His own love toward us, in *that while we were yet sinners,* Christ died for us.—Romans 5:8 (NASB)

When we have our minds set on getting to a particular appointment or a particular event that we have scheduled, we may tend to view interruptions as obstacles that are getting in the way of us reaching our goals. We may even think of them as Satanic attacks preventing us from reaching our purpose.

In reality, these may be the most important events in our day. These "interruptions" may be the events God purposed for us before we were born. So we must change the way we view interruptions. In order to view them correctly, as God's divine appointments, *we must retrain ourselves* to welcome interruptions as appointments with destiny.

In addition, as we retrain ourselves to recognize the significance of interruptions, we must retrain ourselves to *be more "in the moment" and alert* to the realization that these God-ordained appointments may occur at any time, without warning and without any hint that signals their eternal significance. We must be ready to welcome interruptions, *even when they come at the most inconvenient moments, even when they come with bad attitudes, with inappropriate actions and in unexpected ways that might otherwise offend us.*

John Paul Jackson, founder of Streams Ministries, had an experience in which God allowed him to view a day in the life of one believer. It was a day filled with interruptions. In John Paul's experience, he saw this woman going through her day, frustrated at all of the interruptions, but God "pulled back the curtains," so to speak, to allow John Paul to see what was happening in the spiritual realm. He saw how God arranged these so-called "interruptions" to accomplish His will, bring the

Kingdom of God into this believer's environment, and change one cashier's life forever.

In John Paul's experience, the believer was not aware of the flurry of activity in the unseen spiritual realm around her. She was not aware of what God was accomplishing as He masterfully orchestrated circumstances that created apparent "interruptions" for her. She seemed to be simply experiencing a day filled with frustrations and circumstances that were constantly forcing her to adjust and make changes to what she previously planned to do.

I highly recommend that you find the video of John Paul relating this experience and watch it for yourself. You should be able to look it up on the Internet and find it on YouTube. It is called "Storms, Faith & the Miraculous" This story begins about eleven minutes and twenty seconds into Part Two of the four-part video series (Jackson, 2007).

When Roland Buck was taken to the heavenly Throne Room on January 21, 1977, he was given a piece of paper with a list of 120 events that would happen to him in the near future. Upon his return from his heavenly visit, one by one, those events began to happen in order as they were written on the paper.

> In this paper, He didn't tell me that He was putting down everything that would happen. He said, "I just want to pick out a few things so you can see by confirmation that God is really on the job." So, undoubtedly, there were hundreds of things in between each of these events, but He let me see just a few to have as markers along the road.

> I've had people ask me, "Well what about the 120? When they're all done, what's going to happen then?" And I just let them know that it's all planned out ahead of that just as much as we'll find on the other side, only I don't know about it. (Buck, 1979)

You can listen to Roland Buck relate this story, and many others, in his recorded sermons available at www.angelsonassignment.org. I suggest that you start with the titles, "I Visited the Throne Room" and "Sequel to the Throne Room."

If we can get a glimpse of how God orchestrates the seemingly insignificant circumstances of our lives on a daily basis, we would feel a great sense of security and peace, knowing that God has *everything* under control. We would also be struck with a compulsion to become more alert to what God is doing in our lives from moment to moment so that we can cooperate with Him rather than working against what He is doing.

But what if some interruptions really are Satanic attacks? Should we even view *problems* that come into our lives as God's will and *thank* Him for them? If we could see what waits on the other side, we would!

> Consider it pure joy, my brothers and sisters, whenever you face trials of many kinds, because you know that the testing of your faith produces perseverance. Let perseverance finish its work so that you may be mature and complete, not lacking anything. If any of you lacks wisdom, you should ask God, who gives generously to all without finding fault, and it will be given to you.—James 1:2–5 (NIV)

If we feel that we are unable to rejoice in the midst of problems, James tells us that it is because of a lack of wisdom—that we are not seeing the circumstances as God sees them. We ask for wisdom so that we are able to see our problems as opportunities for God to do mighty works on our behalf.

You may be thinking, "But you don't know what my problems are!" That may be true, but have any of us ever had a bigger problem than Jesus did when He was condemned to die on the cross? That's a big problem, right? But Scripture tells us that if the forces of darkness understood what would result from that, they would have never arranged for that to happen. They arranged it, but they will regret it for eternity!

> But we speak the wisdom of God in a mystery, even the hidden wisdom, which God ordained before the world unto our glory: Which none of the princes of this world knew: for had they known it, they would not have crucified the Lord of glory.—1Corinthians 2:7–9 (KJV)

It is the same with you. Satan may orchestrate attacks upon you. *Thank God when you find yourself in those circumstances* because of the great victory that God will bring about as a result of it. That is what Jesus told us to do in the Sermon on the Mount (Matthew 5:11–12); and it is how the early disciples responded when they faced very difficult problems (Colossians 1:24; 1 Peter 1:6–8); and it is how the apostles exhorted us to respond in every situation (1 Thessalonians 5:16).

> Give thanks in all circumstances; for this is God's will for you in Christ Jesus.—1 Thessalonians 5:18 (NIV)

> For I reckon that the sufferings of this present time are not worthy to be compared with the glory which shall be revealed in us.—Romans 8:18 (KJV)

> Beloved, do not be surprised at the fiery ordeal among you, which comes upon you for your testing, as though some strange thing were happening to you; but to the degree that you share the sufferings of Christ, keep on rejoicing, so that also at the revelation of His glory you may rejoice with exultation.—1 Peter 4:12–13 (NASB)

Remember Job? God restored to him twice as much as he lost when Satan attacked him.

> And the Lord turned the captivity of Job and restored his fortunes, when he prayed for his friends; also the Lord gave Job twice as much as he had before...And the Lord blessed the latter days of Job more than his beginning...—Job 42:10–12a (AMP)

Remember Daniel, who was thrown into the lions' den? This event was certainly a big, unwelcome interruption in Daniel's plans, but through it all, he kept his focus on God. He had complete confidence that God was in control of his circumstances. He didn't complain or curse the people responsible for putting him in this tough situation. In fact, the first words out of Daniel's mouth after surviving a night in the lions' den were a blessing upon the king who had put him there!

This unwelcome, unpleasant interruption in Daniel's life resulted in a decree being sent out to everyone in the kingdom of the Medes and Persians, glorifying God and *commanding* that people everywhere honor the God of Daniel! But it didn't end there. This story is still repeated today, all over the world, and continues to bring glory to God to this day!

And it's all because of one interruption in one man's life!

Think of Shadrach, Meshach, and Abednego. They were thrown into a fiery furnace. *Big* interruption in their plans, right? But they verbally acknowledged to the king their complete confidence that God was in control of their circumstances.

> If we are thrown into the blazing furnace, the God we serve is able to deliver us from it, and he will deliver us from Your Majesty's hand. But even if he does not, we want you to

know, Your Majesty, that we will not serve your gods or worship the image of gold you have set up.—Daniel 3:17–18 (NIV)

As a result of this "interruption" in their lives, the king of Babylon (the most powerful man in the world at that time) verbally glorified God and sent out a decree to everyone in his kingdom that no one should speak a negative word against the God of Shadrach, Meshach, and Abednego. He also personally promoted all three men to important positions of responsibility in the kingdom of Babylon.

All because of one interruption in the lives of these men.

And what about Joseph? His life as the favored son was cruelly interrupted when he was first tossed into a pit by his own brothers, sold into slavery, falsely accused, and then thrown into prison! But in the midst of all of these interruptions, Joseph had confidence that God was in complete control of these circumstances in his life. After he was promoted to the position of second most powerful man in Egypt (and eventually in the world because of the famine), he was reunited with the brothers who had brought about these life-altering interruptions in his life. This was Joseph's response:

You intended to harm me, but God intended it for good to accomplish what is now being done, the saving of many lives.—Genesis 50:20 (NIV)

But what if the interruption is so severe that it results in death, as in the lives of Jesus or Stephen? That is when we can truly experience the miracle of exponential multiplication of our impact for the kingdom of God! As Jesus said, "Truly, truly, I say to you, unless a grain of wheat falls into the earth and dies, it remains alone; but if it dies, it bears much fruit." (John 12:24 ESV)

When Jesus' life and ministry were "interrupted" or "cut off," as it reads in Daniel 9:26, it was the best thing that could have happened for the impact of his life and ministry! Because of His death, the veil of separation between God and man was torn apart forever, and the way of salvation was opened for all of us!

Jesus did not look upon His death at a young age as a negative thing. He saw the blessings that would result in it for all of us! He also realized that His death would allow us to experience the Holy Spirit in ways that were never before possible!

> But I tell you the truth, it is to your advantage that I go away; for if I do not go away, the Helper will not come to you; but if I go, I will send Him to you.—John 16:7 (NASB)

But that was Jesus. He was special, wasn't He? Can good things come out of the death of an ordinary person?

Paul Keith Davis, founder of WhiteDove Ministries, had a revelation about the death of Stephen. In Paul Keith's revelation, after the devil persuaded people to take Stephen's life in Acts 7, the Lord took one of Satan's stars, Saul of Tarsus, in exchange. As Paul the Apostle, he probably did more damage to the kingdom of darkness than Stephen ever would have in his lifetime.

Paul Keith Davis has related this revelation in several of his messages. You can search for it on YouTube. It is included, for example, about nineteen minutes into the Saturday Morning Session at New Life Christian Church in Rice Lake, Wisconsin, from August 20, 2011. (Davis, 2011)

The devil never wins. Sometimes we think he wins because our focus is too narrow. In many, many instances, death was not the end of the story. On the contrary, out of death came the greatest harvest and the greatest blessings!

Consider Rachel Scott, one of the first students killed in the Columbine tragedy. Her desire was to reach multitudes of people with the love of Christ. Her funeral, which included many testimonies to the goodness of God, was televised uninterrupted by CNN and seen around the world by more people than any other broadcast on that station, eclipsing even Princess Diana's funeral. Rachel's influence still lives on and is growing through the Rachel's Challenge organization and other movements, impacting the lives of literally millions of people. (Scott, Nimmo, & Rabey, 2000)

Satan never wins. He can't win. He just keeps trying the same things over and over; and God keeps turning those things around for good in the lives of everyone who loves Him and is called according to His purpose (Romans 8:28).

Learn to cooperate with what God is doing in your life. When you complain about your circumstances and take matters into your own hands, you take them *out* of God's hands.

Discipleship Practice:
Seeing Interruptions as God Sees Them

Objective: To become more alert to God's divine appointments

How often? Daily for three weeks or until it becomes a habit

Instead of viewing interruptions as obstacles that keep us from our goals, begin to view these "interruptions" as God's divine appointments.

- Every morning thank God for the interruptions that will occur throughout your day. Thank Him for interrupting your schedule with His divine appointments.

- Prepare yourself every morning by asking God to help you respond correctly and not be offended by the following:

  o inconvenient interruptions

  o people with bad attitudes

  o people who act inappropriately

- When interruptions happen, thank God, even when the interruptions seem to cause problems. (1 Thessalonians 5:18)

- Keep a small notebook, and record the interruptions that occurred during your day.

- At the end of the day, think back on one or two interruptions that happened and ask God what His purposes were for them. Was there more that God wanted to accomplish in these encounters? Could you have responded in a way that better demonstrated God's love?

Years after I had started practicing this discipleship exercise, I was astounded to read this account by Dale Carnegie of a Wall Street bank president who practiced something very similar to this on a weekly basis:

The president of an important Wall Street bank once described, in a talk before one of my classes, a highly efficient system he used for self-improvement. This man had little formal schooling; yet he had become one of the most important financiers in America, and he confessed that he owed most of his success to the constant application of his homemade system. This is what he does. I'll put it in his own words as accurately as I can remember.

For years I have kept an engagement book showing all the appointments I had during the day. My family never made any plans for me on Saturday night, for the family knew that I devoted a part of each Saturday evening to the illuminating process of self-examination and review and appraisal. After dinner I went off by myself, opened my engagement book, and thought over all the interviews, discussions and meetings that had taken place during the week. I asked myself:

What mistakes did I make that time?

What did I do that was right—and in what way could I have improved my performance?

What lessons can I learn from that experience?

I often found that this weekly review made me very unhappy. I was frequently astonished at my own blunders. Of course, as the years passed, these blunders became less frequent. Sometimes I was inclined to pat myself on the back a little after one of these sessions. This system of self-analysis, self-education, continued year after year, did more for me than any other one thing I have ever attempted.

It helped me improve my ability to make decisions—and it aided me enormously in all my contacts with people. I cannot recommend it too highly. (Carnegie, 1936)

We must retrain ourselves to be alert to the realization that these God-ordained appointments may occur at any time, without warning and without any hint that signals their eternal significance.

Significant opportunities for ministry come and go in seconds. And they often come disguised as interruptions...with bad attitudes...acting inappropriately.

But God demonstrates His own love toward us, in that while we were yet sinners, Christ died for us.—Romans 5:8 (NASB)

Walking with God

When we begin to thank God for every circumstance and interruption in our lives, and pray into them at the end of the day, something wonderful begins to happen. He begins to speak to us about future events in our lives, as well as giving meaning to things that we have already experienced, and we begin to *walk with God*.

Howbeit when he, the Spirit of truth, is come, he will guide you into all truth: for he shall not speak of himself; but whatsoever he shall hear, that shall he speak: and *he will shew you things to come.*—John 16:13 (KJV)

It may be just a taste, not yet a moment-by-moment experience, but we definitely begin to walk *with* God through our lives, experiencing circumstances with *Him*, as He shares His point of view with us. This occurs because, finally, instead of complaining about the circumstances that God brings into our lives and rejecting them and fighting against them, we accept and embrace them. In doing that, we come into agreement with what God is doing in our lives.

Until we come into agreement with what God is doing in our lives, embrace it and accept it with thankfulness, we cannot fully walk with God.

Can two walk together, except they be agreed?—Amos 3:3 (KJV)

On the other hand, God will only put up with a limited amount of complaining before He has had enough.

Nor discontentedly complain as some of them did—and were put out of the way entirely by the destroyer (death). Now these things befell them by way of a figure [as an example and warning to us].—1 Corinthians 10:10–11a (AMP)

God took personal responsibility for the difficult circumstances that the children of Israel faced as they journeyed in the wilderness. When they complained about those circumstances, He took it personally. They were complaining about Him. He listened to their complaints for only a limited amount of time before he turned them over to the destroyer, who ended their lives. First Corinthians 10:11 makes it clear that this was not an isolated event. Their judgment is a warning to us. If we gripe and complain about the circumstances that God brings into our lives in the same way they did, we shouldn't be surprised to experience consequences similar to what they experienced.

With Every Concept, Balance Is Needed

Having a willingness to welcome interruptions as divine appointments does not mean that we allow others to take advantage of us and steer us out of the path God has called us to walk. That was disastrous for the unnamed man of God in 1 Kings 13.

This man delivered a powerful prophecy to King Jeroboam. Then, as he was traveling back home, an old prophet met him and invited him to his house. He told the old prophet that God had warned him not to eat or drink and not to go home the same way he came. The old prophet lied and said an angel had told him to bring him to his house. After the man of God ate and drank with the old prophet, he was killed by a lion on his way home.

Jesus welcomed interruptions but balanced that approach with discretion and never surrendered his destiny to the will of another.

> But Jesus did not commit Himself to them, because He knew all men, and had no need that anyone should testify of man, for He knew what was in man.—John 2:24–25 (NKJV)

The Gospels contain several examples of times when Jesus either said "no" to people who would have led Him out of the path He was called to walk, or when he sent people away in order to be able to pursue God as He was called to do.

> And when *He had sent them away*, He departed to the mountain to pray.—Mark 6:46 (NKJV)

> Now those who had eaten were about four thousand. And *He sent them away.*—Mark 8:9 (NKJV)

> Therefore when Jesus perceived that they were about to come and take Him by force to make Him king, *He departed again to the mountain by Himself alone.*—John 6:15 (NKJV)

As another example, when Jesus began to reveal things to His disciples about his coming crucifixion, Peter took Him aside and began to rebuke Him, saying, "Far be it from You, Lord; this shall not happen to You!" But He turned and said to Peter, "Get behind Me, Satan! You are an offense to Me, for you are not mindful of the things of God, but the things of men."—Matthew 16:21–23 (NKJV)

When He returned from His intense times of solitary prayer, He was always alert and ready to respond to people with powerful demonstrations of the love of God, even when they seemed to cause interruptions for Him.

CHAPTER 5
WHO DO WE LOVE?

Who Are We Commanded to Love?

If you believe that we are supposed to love everybody, look again. Surprisingly, God never commanded us to love everybody. That's God's job. He's big enough to handle it.

> For *God so loved the world*, that He gave his only begotten son...—John 3:16 (KJV)

If we were commanded to love *everybody* in the world, that would be overwhelming. How could we ever hope to accomplish that? God never saddled us with that kind of responsibility.

In fact, the only time Jesus even singled out a *group* of people for us to love was in His command to "love your enemies" (Matthew 5:44; Luke 6:27). *In every other case*, He commanded us to direct our love to *individuals*—to focus on the *one* near us who has needs. That is manageable. That is something we can handle. And that is where He wants our focus to be.

These things I command you, that you love *one another*.—
John 15:17

You shall love *your neighbor* as yourself.–Matthew 19:19;
Matthew 22:39; Mark 12:31; Luke 10:27

A new commandment I give to you, that you love *one another*; as I have loved you, that you also love *one another*. By this all will know that you are My disciples, if you have love for *one another*.–John 13:34-35

This is My commandment, that you love *one another* as I have loved you. Greater love has no one than this, than to lay down one's life for his friends.–John 15: 12–13

So...Who Is the Focus of Our Ministry?

God wants the focus of our ministry to be on individuals we encounter who have needs.

Jesus gave us a clear picture of what this looks like in the story of the Good Samaritan in Luke 10:25–37.

Notice that when the Samaritan stopped to help the man in need, he was on his way to go somewhere else. This was an interruption in his schedule.

We are called and commanded to be "neighbors" who show mercy to individuals who have needs. Jesus finished this story of the Good Samaritan by saying, "Go and do thou likewise."

As Heidi Baker often says, "Just love the one in front of you."

"I Send You Out"

When Jesus commissioned his disciples, he did *not* send them into churches. Jesus sent them *out* into the cities and towns, after His example.

Picture this. You're in the greatest Bible school that has ever existed. Jesus Christ Himself is the head of the Bible school, and He is the teacher of all the subjects. When it comes time for your internship/apprenticeship, you might expect that He would set you up in some cushy position in a prominent church as an associate pastor or maybe a youth minister. Nope. Jesus sent them *out*—into the cities and towns, after His example, and then He followed them and went to those same cities and towns with His ministry (Matthew 10:1–16; Mark 3:13–15; 6:7–13; Luke 9:1–6; 10:1–17). Sending His disciples out also reinforces the observation that the focus of Jesus' ministry was on encounters outside of traditional church meetings.

> The seventy returned with joy, saying, Lord, even the demons are subject to us in Your name!—Luke 10:17 (AMP)

For decades, our main evangelistic strategy in America has been to invite people to come to church. The unspoken rationale has been that, if we can just get people to venture inside the church, *then* they will receive the ministry that they need. The church will "fix them."

But doing things Jesus' way, we get marvelous results when we simply follow Jesus' model and go *out* to minister. In my experience, I've been blessed with opportunities to minister alongside wonderful believers who went into festivals and conventions (and almost any other gathering of people) to share God's love with others. In those settings, we would usually set up a booth or plant ourselves in a particular location and minister to people who came our way.

When we have followed Jesus' model for ministry outside of church meetings, we have consistently had so many people lined up for ministry that we have had difficulty meeting the demand! We tend to lose count of all of the salvations, healings, and deliverances that take place in these outreach settings, but we've got books full of wonderful, memorable testimonies!

Instead of simply inviting people to church, Jesus commands us to take "church" to them (Matthew 28:19–20).

In a meeting at Sojourn Church in Dallas, Texas, I heard John Paul Jackson say, "I was raised in church. I've been going to church all my life, but I saw who God was when I went to the streets." This is from a man who, at that time, had been in full-time ministry for twenty-eight years!

As the Father Draws Them

We have noticed that when people come to us in outreach settings, they tend to open up to us. They let their defensive "walls" and barriers down. They share openly with us about their problems and needs, volunteering to be vulnerable.

I believe this sense of trust develops—at least in part—because they sense that we have *no agenda* for the encounters. We are not trying to push them in any particular direction.

There is no sense in pushing people to make a decision they are not ready to make because we understand that "No one is able to come to Me [Jesus] unless the Father Who sent Me attracts and draws him and gives him the desire to come to Me..." (John 6:44 AMP)

In fact, there is danger in pushing someone into a premature decision. It can actually delay their journey to salvation and make it harder for them to come to Jesus. Jesus warned us clearly of this in Matthew 12:30 (NKJV):

He who is not with Me is against Me, and he who does not gather with Me scatters abroad.

It is crucial for us to work *in cooperation* with what God is doing in a person's life, *not against it.* If we work in cooperation with the Lord, we will see signs that confirm that.

And they went out and preached everywhere, the Lord working with them and confirming the word through the accompanying signs.—Mark 16:20 (NKJV)

If instead, we push people in a direction God is not leading them at this time, we will experience frustration, resistance, and rejection; and even if they make a momentary decision as a result of our insistence, there is real danger that it will be short-lived because it was *our* decision, not *theirs.* They may quickly fall away, and it will be much, much more difficult for them to be drawn back to Jesus. This is precisely Jesus' warning to us in Matthew 12:30: "He who does not gather with Me scatters abroad."

Finding people who have been "scattered abroad" is easy. Just ask people what they think about Jesus. If they have a negative reaction to the name of Jesus, ask them why. Most likely they will recount negative experiences with Christians that have turned them away from Jesus and away from the Christian Church. They have been "scattered abroad."

Their previous negative experiences with Christians will actually compound the difficulty for them to be drawn to Jesus.

Why is it that when people see a street preacher, they often cross over to the other side of the street to avoid him, but mobs of people flocked around Jesus wherever He went? What was it about Jesus' ministry that drew people to Him, and what is it about some of our ministry that drives people away?

As you read of Jesus' evangelistic encounters with people in the four Gospels, take time to notice that *Jesus never pushed anyone into a decision.*

He never experienced resistance to an invitation because He never pushed people in a direction into which they were not already being drawn.

You never read of Jesus using persuasive arguments to bring a person to a decision to accept Him as Lord and Savior, persistently urging the person to make a decision *now*, before he or she leaves His presence.

It was not His way then, and it is not His way now. He was there to support and guide people on their journey, but He never pushed them into a decision.

Consider these examples:

- Jesus called the first disciples with a single, simple invitation: "Follow Me." (Matthew 9:9; Mark 2:14; John 1:43)

- Nathaniel made his confession of faith without any urging or prompting from Jesus. (John 1:49)

- The woman at the well was not *pushed* to confess Jesus as Messiah. (John 4:29)

- Peter was allowed to follow Jesus for months before he finally made a confession of faith (Matthew 16:13; Mark 8:27; Luke 9:21).

- Jesus did not force His ministry on the man at the pool of Bethesda. Jesus first asked, "Do you want to be healed?" (John 5:6)

- Neither did Jesus force His ministry on Blind Bartimaeus. He asked, "What do you want Me to do for you?" (Mark 10:51)

- Jesus didn't even try to talk Judas out of the worst decision of his life—betraying Jesus to death.

Jesus never forced His ministry on anyone. In fact, there were times that He actually refused to help people who asked—at least at first.

Sometimes He said "no" to ministry because He believed the timing was not right, as with His mother, Mary, at the wedding in Cana. "Dear woman, why do you bring me into this?" Jesus replied. "My time has not yet come."—John 2:4 (NIRV)

Other times he refused to minister because He believed it was outside of what He was called to do, as with the Syro-Phoenician woman. "He answered, 'I was sent only to the lost sheep of the house of Israel...It is not right to take the children's bread and throw it to the dogs."—Matthew 15:24–26 (ESV)

If persuasion and hard-sell techniques are the way to go, why not go back to the methods of the military religious crusades of the twelfth century? "Confess Jesus Christ as Lord and Savior now, or I will chop your head off!" If we take hard-sell approaches to their logical extreme, that is what we would get.

Accepted Just as They Are

During our ministry encounters with people outside the walls of the church, we build rapport. We accept and love people as they are. We don't require them to change in any way before we minister to their needs.

We may tend to think that we must first address sin in someone's life before ministry may take place, but this was not Jesus' way.

- He healed people without requiring them to repent first.

- He fed the five thousand without requiring them to repent first.

- Even when confronted with sin directly, as with the woman taken in adultery, He did not require repentance before He demonstrated His love for her. When He did address sin, it was from a view of what was in her best interest. "Neither do I condemn you; go and sin no more."—John 8:11 (NKJV)

- In the same way, he addressed sin in the life of the man who was at the Bethesda pool only *after* He met his need and healed him. "See, you have been made well. Sin no more, lest a worse thing come upon you."—John 5:14 (NKJV)

A few years ago, during the annual Haunted Happenings festival in Salem, Massachusetts, I was part of a ministry team when a woman came to us for help and encouragement. As we waited on the Holy Spirit, I had a vision of a picture-perfect home with a nice, white picket fence around it. Then an enormous butcher knife came down and sliced the whole scene in half—an image of a broken home. I asked her if she had experienced the pain of a broken home. The lady shared with us that she had just gone through a divorce—with her female partner. As she related the story, tears welled up in her eyes. The pain was still very close to the surface.

It became clear to us that what was on God's heart for that woman, that night, was to bring healing to her broken heart, meeting her in the place of her need and dealing with the devastating effects of a broken home. At no time that night did the Holy Spirit prompt us to persuade her to renounce her lifestyle.

Love, acceptance, healing—meeting needs without conditions or prerequisites. Those qualities characterized Jesus' ministry when He walked on earth, and those same qualities must characterize our lives and ministries as well.

> He causes his sun to shine on evil people and good people. He sends rain on those who do right and those who don't. If you love those who love you, what reward will you get? Even the tax collectors do that. If you greet only your own people, what more are you doing than others? Even people who are ungodly do that. So be perfect, just as your Father in heaven is perfect.—Matthew 5:45–48 (NIRV)

My New Best Friend

To put myself in the right frame of mind, I think of the person coming to me for ministry as *my new best friend*. Thinking this way helps me to build instant rapport with those I encounter. In that frame of mind, I immediately like them. I want to understand them. I want to do what I can to help them.

> Then Jesus, looking at him, *loved him*, and said to him...—Mark 10:21a (NKJV)

During encounters with people, we begin to *form relationships* by *demonstrating* sincere care and concern and a willingness to help people through their problems—a willingness to help them find the answers they are looking for.

After our ministry encounters, we often invite people to stay with us, hang out, and join us for meals. *Discipleship is birthed.* Discipleship can begin immediately, during the initial encounter, and be ongoing from that point.

I was thinking about this near the end of one of our week-long outreaches at an extreme, radical, very non-Christian festival. Many of those who had received ministry during the week stayed around to join us at mealtimes.

Speaking with one of our leaders, I said, "You know, I feel like we are medics on a battlefield. There are wounded people all around us, and we are scrambling to get to them and bind up their wounds and bring healing and help to them." After I related that feeling, I remembered this passage from Luke. The comment in parentheses is my own:

> And there were a great number of tax collectors and others who sat down with them. And their scribes and the Pharisees complained against His disciples, saying, "Why do You eat and drink with tax collectors and sinners?" Jesus answered and said to them, "Those who are well have no need of a physician (or maybe a medic?), but those who are sick. I have not come to call the righteous, but sinners, to repentance.—Luke 5:29–32 (NKJV)

As we began to follow Jesus' model for ministry, we began to experience similar results to those that Jesus experienced.

Father Greg Boyle shares similar experiences in his dealings with Los Angeles gang members:

> If you read Scripture scholar Marcus Borg and go to the index in search of "sinner," it'll say, "see outcast." This was a social grouping of people who felt wholly unacceptable. The world had deemed them disgraceful and shameful, and this toxic shame, as I have mentioned before, was brought inside and given a home in the outcast.

> Jesus' strategy is a simple one: He eats with them. Precisely to those paralyzed in this toxic shame, Jesus says, "I will eat with you." He goes where love has not yet arrived, and he

"gets his grub on." Eating with outcasts rendered them acceptable. (Boyle, 2010)

We weren't too concerned about the level of commitment exhibited by the people who hung out with us after ministry. Jesus allowed *anyone* to follow Him initially, but at some point in the journey, each person had to count the cost and make an individual choice either to commit everything to Jesus and become a true disciple or to turn back and return to his or her old lifestyle. Everyone will come to a point of no return somewhere along the path.

Look on the Fields

In some outreach events, we consistently have people lined up, waiting for their chance to receive ministry, sometimes waiting for over an hour in unpleasant conditions. Commonly, when we offer apologies for the long wait, they respond by saying something like, "That's OK. I heard it was worth it."

When we simply follow Jesus' model for ministry *outside* of church meetings, we often have so many people line up to receive prayer, healing, encouraging prophetic words, and other forms of ministry that we have difficulty meeting the demand.

In contrast, our experiences in church meetings are often nothing like this. Why, instead, is church membership in America down overall? Why do people often view church attendance as a chore or an unpleasant duty?

When I come back from an outreach event where we had difficulty meeting the consistently high demand for ministry, I hear people in churches and on Christian TV and radio praying earnestly for God to send a revival. I can't help but feel that I just came back from "the revival"—but it wasn't inside the Church. It was *outside*, among the people with needs.

I have experienced two extended revivals in Spirit-filled churches. In both cases, God blessed His people in wonderful ways. There were healings, deliverances, salvation, and other wonderful blessings. At the same time, as the days of continuous revival meetings wore on and volunteers were asked to attend and help in various ways night after night after night, exhaustion and even disillusionment set in; and as the length of the revival increased, fewer and fewer church members attended the meetings.

In contrast, when groups come back and share testimonies from mission trips, they seem unanimously enthusiastic, energized, and eager to go back as soon as it can be scheduled! "The seventy returned with joy, saying, Lord, even the demons are subject to us in Your name!"—Luke 10:17 (AMP)

Why the difference?

In my experience, exhaustion can be a signal that I am involved in something that God is not giving grace for me to do. This is not always the case. Sometimes, even though the motivation is there, I am just tired and need to rest before continuing.

God's grace brings with it the desire, the motivation, and the energy to accomplish His will.

So, if volunteering in church revival meetings leaves me exhausted and disillusioned, *but* going *outside the church* and ministering together with a team leaves me energized and wanting more, maybe God is trying to tell me something.

While we pray earnestly for revival to come to the church, and hopefully encourage each other by telling ourselves that when the anointing comes—maybe in a few months' time—revival will explode in our church, maybe Jesus is saying this instead:

You say, 'Four months more, and then it will be harvest time.' But I tell you, open your eyes! Look at the fields! They are ripe for harvest right now."—John 4:35 (NIRV)

Could it be...that if we will just *go out*, like Jesus did, it will happen, and we will begin to experience results similar to those that Jesus saw in His ministry? I believe the answer is *yes*!

CHAPTER 6
HOW DO WE PREPARE?

The Greater the Darkness,
The Greater the Anointing

In Jesus' ministry, part of the reason for His great impact was the contrast of bringing such great light into a place of such great darkness.

> The people who sat (dwelt enveloped) in darkness have seen a great Light, and for those who sat in the land and shadow of death Light has dawned.—Matthew 4:16 (AMP)

We are commanded to do the same thing.

> In the same way, let your light shine before others, so that they may see your good works and give glory to your Father who is in heaven.—Matthew 5:16 (ESV)

There are definite advantages in taking ministry outside the walls of the Church. God gives us incentives for doing this. Along with impacting people with God's love, we grow exponentially in authority, strength, favor, confidence, and expertise in the skills of ministry because God's anointing increases as we go out to minister.

In July, 2009, I was in Scotland, waiting for a meeting to begin during the CLAN Gathering conference. While I was waiting, I chatted with the gentleman in front of me. During our chat, he spoke a prophetic word over me, saying that I would enter into Ezekiel 47, experiencing it in my life. That chapter speaks of Ezekiel being led into deeper and deeper water as he went farther and farther away from the temple.

Our conversation was cut short because the meeting was getting underway. The speaker at that meeting was Heidi Baker. Amazingly enough, her message for that meeting was based on Ezekiel 47! She invited us to experience this passage of Scripture, and even had blue silken banners (representing deep water) lifted over our heads, covering us, as a prophetic act of entering into this Scriptural experience.

The principle of Ezekiel 47:1–10 is that the further away we go, outside of the traditional church meetings, into the darkness, the deeper the waters will be. The depth of the waters here indicates the level of the Holy Spirit's anointing, revelation, and power for ministry.

> Then he brought me back to the door of the temple; and there was water, flowing from under the threshold of the temple toward the east, for the front of the temple faced east; the water was flowing from under the right side of the temple, south of the altar. He brought me out by way of the north gate, and led me around on the outside to the outer gateway that faces east; and there was water, running out on the right side. And when the man went out to the east with the line in his hand, he measured one thousand cubits, and he brought me through the waters; the water came up to my ankles. Again he measured one thousand and brought

me through the waters; the water came up to my knees. Again he measured one thousand and brought me through; the water came up to my waist. Again he measured one thousand, and it was a river that I could not cross; for the water was too deep, water in which one must swim, a river that could not be crossed...

And it shall be that every living thing that moves, wherever the rivers go, will live. There will be a very great multitude of fish, because these waters go there; for they will be healed, and everything will live wherever the river goes. It shall be that fishermen will stand by it from En Gedi to En Eglaim; they will be places for spreading their nets. Their fish will be of the same kinds as the fish of the Great Sea, exceedingly many.—Ezekiel 47:1–10 (NKJV)

Multiple sources report that through Heidi Baker's ministry in Africa:

• Ten thousand churches have been started. (Stafford, 2012)

• Thousands of people are fed *every day.* (Baker & Baker, 2003)

• Countless people have been healed. (Stafford, 2012)

• At least fifty-three people have been raised from the dead. (Grady)

Why is it that Heidi Baker's ministry in Mozambique has seen so many of these types of extraordinary miracles, but we are not seeing the same things in our churches? Could it be because she obeyed to go into the darkness of Mozambique? She is swimming in deep water now, isn't she?

Going Into the Darkness Is Not Enough

But just going into the darkness is not enough. Remember the seven sons of Sceva?

Some Jews who went around driving out evil spirits tried to invoke the name of the Lord Jesus over those who were demon-possessed. They would say, "In the name of the Jesus whom Paul preaches, I command you to come out."

Seven sons of Sceva, a Jewish chief priest, were doing this. One day the evil spirit answered them, "Jesus I know, and Paul I know about, but who are you?" Then the man who had the evil spirit jumped on them and overpowered them all. He gave them such a beating that they ran out of the house naked and bleeding. When this became known to the Jews and Greeks living in Ephesus, they were all seized with fear, and the name of the Lord Jesus was held in high honor.—Acts 19:13–20 (NIV)

We must be prepared, and we must have a strategy. When we go into dark places, like Heidi Baker did, how can we be sure that we won't end up like the sons of Sceva?

Preparation

Appropriate preparation is essential. Jesus did not send out the twelve on the first day of their discipleship; and He did not send them out without detailed, specific instruction. At least five aspects of preparation are needed to ensure victory upon being sent out into the darkness:

1. Equipping
2. Training

3. Practice
4. Confidence
5. Availability

Let's examine these five aspects in a little more detail.

Preparation Piece 1: Equipping

Equipping is acquiring the power and tools needed for effective, victorious ministry. Equipping is a work of the Holy Spirit and may be imparted by church leadership through the laying on of hands. Equipping is impartation of the Spirit of God and spiritual gifts. Jesus imparted power to His disciples before He sent them out.

> And Jesus summoned to Him His twelve disciples and gave them power and authority over unclean spirits, to drive them out, and to cure all kinds of disease and all kinds of weakness and infirmity.—Matthew 10:1 (AMP)

> And He called to Him the Twelve [apostles] and began to send them out [as His ambassadors] two by two and gave them authority and power over the unclean spirits.—Mark 6:7 (AMP)

> Then Jesus called together the Twelve [apostles] and gave them power and authority over all demons, and to cure diseases, and He sent them out to announce and preach the kingdom of God and to bring healing.—Luke 9:1,2 (AMP)

> The seventy returned with joy, saying, Lord, even the demons are subject to us in Your name! And He said to them, I saw Satan falling like a lightning [flash] from heaven. Behold! I have given you authority and power to

trample upon serpents and scorpions, and [physical and mental strength and ability] over all the power that the enemy [possesses]; and nothing shall in any way harm you.—Luke 10:17–19 (AMP)

After Jesus' resurrection, the disciples were instructed to wait in Jerusalem before they ventured out, so that they would be endued with power. In Acts 1, Jesus made it clear that this power would come through the baptism in the Holy Spirit. He also indicated that the baptism in the Holy Spirit was necessary *before* they could be effective witnesses for Him.

I am going to send you what my Father has promised. But for now, stay in the city. Stay there until you have received power from heaven.—Luke 24:49 (NIRV)

One day Jesus was eating with them. He gave them a command. "Do not leave Jerusalem," he said. "Wait for the gift my Father promised. You have heard me talk about it. John baptized with water. But in a few days you will be baptized with the Holy Spirit...you will receive power when the Holy Spirit comes on you. Then you will be my witnesses in Jerusalem. You will be my witnesses in all Judea and Samaria. And you will be my witnesses from one end of the earth to the other.—Acts 1:4–8 (NIRV)

Years ago, I was attending a Streams Ministries conference in the Boston area. Thursday night was a special night for partners of the ministry. At the end of the meeting, John Paul Jackson hugged each one of us and prayed for us to receive an impartation from the Holy Spirit. When he came to me, John Paul gave me one of his characteristic bear hugs and prayed for me to receive gifts of signs and wonders according to my heart's desire...or something like that. I don't remember the exact words he used.

The next day, there was a special luncheon for partners of the ministry. I happened to sit at a table with people whom I had not met before, but we enjoyed getting to know one another. On my left sat Emily and her friend Mary, who was a pastor's wife.

I ran into Mary again later. In between conference sessions, as I was making my way from one meeting room to another, Mary saw me in the hallway and turned back to another lady, saying, "Here he is! Here is the man I was telling you about!"

Mary explained her reaction by telling me that when we had been sitting together at the luncheon table, *my hands were on fire*! She said that every time she looked at my hands, she saw bright orange flames coming from my hands!

She told me that she had not said anything about it while we were sitting together because, based on our reactions, the rest of us didn't see it, and she didn't want us to think she was crazy! This was even more remarkable because she told me that she had never seen a supernatural vision before. For me, this was confirmation that I had received a significant spiritual impartation from John Paul.

I had not seen the "flaming hands," nor had I felt anything after John Paul prayed for me, but I had obviously received something powerful! I learned that day that, just because I don't *feel* anything after prayer, it doesn't mean that I didn't *receive*!

The Purpose of Church Leaders

Years ago, I sat in a theater and listened with the rest of the audience as a prominent deliverance minister told us story after story of how he had dramatically delivered people from the influences of dark spirits. After listening to several of these stories, I found myself wanting to shout, "Enough stories! Teach me how to do that!" I didn't want to just hear stories about dramatic deliverances. I wanted to be equipped to do that myself!

A word to church leaders:

If, as church leaders, we are doing most of the work of the ministry ourselves, we may be missing our calling. Church leaders are given to the church to *equip others* to do the work of the ministry.

> And His gifts were [varied; He Himself appointed and gave men to us] some to be apostles (special messengers), some prophets (inspired preachers and expounders), some evangelists (preachers of the Gospel, traveling missionaries), some pastors (shepherds of His flock) and teachers. His intention was the perfecting *and* the full equipping of the saints (His consecrated people), [that they should do] the work of ministering toward building up Christ's body (the church).—Ephesians 4:11–12 (AMP)

Elders and other leaders in the church can be used to administer the baptism in the Holy Spirit and to impart power, gifts, and anointings to help equip the Body of Christ. In fact, that is one of the main purposes of the five-fold ministry.

> Simon saw that through the laying on of the apostles' hands the Holy Spirit was given.—Acts 8:18 (NKJV)

> Do not neglect the gift which is in you, [that special inward endowment] which was directly imparted to you [by the Holy Spirit] by prophetic utterance when the elders laid

their hands upon you [at your ordination].—1 Timothy 4:14 (AMP)

That is why I would remind you to stir up (rekindle the embers of, fan the flame of, and keep burning) the [gracious] gift of God, [the inner fire] that is in you by means of the laying on of my hands [with those of the elders at your ordination].—2 Timothy 1:6 (AMP)

Preparation Piece 2: Training

Training involves Bible-based instruction from wise teachers who are experienced in Holy Spirit-led ministry.

Wisdom is the principal thing; Therefore get wisdom. And in all your getting, get understanding.—Proverbs 4:7 (NKJV)

Jesus and the Apostle Paul also made it very clear that power, anointing, and enthusiasm are not enough.

We are instructed by the Apostle Peter that we should, by "giving all diligence, add to your faith virtue, to virtue *knowledge*"—2 Peter 1:5 (NKJV).

I bear them witness that they have a [certain] zeal and enthusiasm for God, but it is not enlightened and according to [correct and vital] knowledge.—Romans 10:2 (AMP)

Behold, I send you out as sheep in the midst of wolves. Therefore be wise as serpents and harmless as doves.— Matthew 10:16 (NKJV).

Choose Wise Teachers

Some of this wisdom will come through experience over time, but studying under the watchful care of wise, experienced teachers and mentors can accelerate the acquisition of wisdom.

He who walks with wise men will be wise, but the companion of fools will be destroyed.—Proverbs 13:20 (NKJV).

Obey your spiritual leaders and submit to them [continually recognizing their authority over you], for they are constantly keeping watch over your souls and guarding your spiritual welfare, as men who will have to render an account [of their trust]. [Do your part to] let them do this with gladness and not with sighing and groaning, for that would not be profitable to you [either].—Hebrews 13:17 (AMP)

Do Your Homework

Church leaders can provide us with excellent training, but as individual disciples, it is essential for us also to reinforce that training with individual study and application of Scripture.

Our *teachers* may have a clear and thorough understanding of the principles of successful ministry, but that does not help *us* much until we internalize scriptural truth ourselves and gain firsthand understanding through our own study and practice.

We must be diligent in our personal study of the Scriptures so that we receive our own revelations of truth directly from the Holy Spirit.

Study and be eager and do your utmost to present yourself to God approved (tested by trial), a workman who has no cause to be ashamed, correctly analyzing and accurately dividing [rightly handling and skillfully teaching] the Word of Truth.—2 Timothy 2:15 (AMP)

He is the rewarder of those who earnestly and diligently seek Him [out].—Hebrews 11:6 (AMP)

Preparation Piece 3: Practice

It is wonderful to have gifts, but Jesus expects us to *do something* with the gifts we are given. This is the message of the parable of the talents in Matthew 25:14–30 (NKJV)

"For the kingdom of heaven is like a man traveling to a far country, who called his own servants and delivered his goods to them. And to one he gave five talents, to another two, and to another one, to each according to his own ability; and immediately he went on a journey. Then he who had received the five talents went and traded with them, and made another five talents. And likewise he who had received two gained two more also. But he who had received one went and dug in the ground, and hid his lord's money. After a long time the lord of those servants came and settled accounts with them.

"So he who had received five talents came and brought five other talents, saying, 'Lord, you delivered to me five talents; look, I have gained five more talents besides them.' His lord said to him, 'Well done, good and faithful servant; you were faithful over a few things, I will make you ruler over many things. Enter into the joy of your lord.' He also who had received two talents came and said, 'Lord, you delivered to me two talents; look, I have gained two more talents besides them.' His lord said to him, 'Well done, good and faithful servant; you have been faithful over a few things, I will make you ruler over many things. Enter into the joy of your lord.'

"Then he who had received the one talent came and said, 'Lord, I knew you to be a hard man, reaping where you have not sown, and gathering where you have not scattered seed. And I was afraid, and went and hid your talent in the ground. Look, there you have what is yours.'

"But his lord answered and said to him, 'You wicked and lazy servant, you knew that I reap where I have not sown, and gather where I have not scattered seed. So you ought to have deposited my money with the bankers, and at my coming I would have received back my own with interest. Therefore take the talent from him, and give it to him who has ten talents.

'For to everyone who has, more will be given, and he will have abundance; but from him who does not have, even what he has will be taken away. And cast the unprofitable servant into the outer darkness. There will be weeping and gnashing of teeth.'"

It seems clear that God does not reward us for our gifts. He rewards us for taking the gifts that He has given us and developing them so that we are highly skilled masters at what we do; performing with excellence.

For even though by this time you ought to be teaching others, you actually need someone to teach you over again the very first principles of God's Word. You have come to need milk, not solid food. For everyone who continues to feed on milk is obviously inexperienced and unskilled in the doctrine of righteousness (of conformity to the divine will in purpose, thought, and action), for he is a mere infant [not able to talk yet]! But solid food is for full-grown men, for those whose senses and mental faculties are *trained by practice* to discriminate and distinguish between what is morally good and noble and what is evil and contrary either to divine or human law.—Hebrews 5:12–14 (AMP)

We often admire people who stand out as masters at what they do—athletes, artists, and performers make what they do look so easy. We may dismiss their impressive performances as the results of being blessed with incredible gifts. The truth is that in most cases, though they may have started out with a gift, that was just a *starting point* for them. In most cases, the performers we admire most are also among the hardest-working people in their areas of expertise. They are often the first ones to arrive at work or practice, and they are often the last ones to leave the practice field or the workplace at the end of the day.

People have told me that I have a teaching gift. That may be true, but after earning three college degrees and with more than twenty-five years of experience in public education, I've put a lot of effort into honing that initial gift into a finely tuned skill.

In the same way, if we expect to take the gifts that God has given us and develop them to high levels of skill and expertise, we must allow time and opportunity for practice (Hebrews 5:14). Whether we are speaking of spiritual gifts or math skills, the principle is the same.

"Practice makes perfect," as the saying goes. When a good teacher introduces a new skill in math class, first he will demonstrate it, and then the class will work through a problem, or a few problems, together. Then the teacher will allow time for supervised group practice, giving concentrated attention to any who might need some extra attention. Finally, the teacher will assign math problems to be completed independently. A master teacher understands that all of this practice, in this sequence, is necessary for the students to remember the concepts and to master the skills that have been taught.

Some of the best practice you'll ever experience will be on mission trips and at outreach events. These are great opportunities to lay aside our day-to-day responsibilities and take time to really focus on doing the works of Jesus. It is remarkable how much we can learn, and how much we can grow, by participating in these focused events.

Don't Give Up!

Everybody falls when first learning to walk or to ride a bicycle, but with practice, almost everyone can master these skills. What may have seemed impossibly out of reach on the first attempt becomes second nature in a relatively short time. With regular practice, we can reach such a level of expertise that we do these things without even thinking about them.

The key is to keep going! Don't give up! You will become proficient if you don't quit!

You never overhear babies saying to each other, "I don't think this 'walking' thing is for me. I've tried, and I just don't get it. I keep making mistakes. I keep falling down after just a step or two. I prayed about it, and I just don't think I have that gift."

We can learn valuable lessons about developing our spiritual gifts by watching babies as they are learning to walk. They may fall over and over and over, but they don't give those falls a second thought. They just get up and try it again, and before we know it, they have mastered the skill of walking unassisted, and they don't even remember all of the spills they took on their way to becoming highly skilled walkers.

A Word to Leaders

As parents, we would never take a bicycle away from our children if they fell once or twice. That's all part of learning. They may take some rough spills before they learn to ride skillfully, but if they do not give up, they will improve rapidly and soon master the skill of riding the bicycle.

As church leaders, we must apply the same principle as we provide guidance to believers who are learning to master the spiritual gifts as well.

Mistakes are a part of learning. In order to facilitate "the perfecting and the full equipping of the saints (His consecrated people), [that they should do] the work of ministering" (Ephesians 4:12 AMP), we must give the saints the freedom to make mistakes and experience some failures along the way, picking them back up, dusting them off, and encouraging them to continue and not give up.

For a righteous man falls seven times and rises again—Proverbs 24:16a (AMP).

Preparation Piece 4: Confidence

Many, many people are equipped and well-trained, but are useless in ministry because lack of confidence keeps them bound in fear. They won't step out for fear of failure or rejection.

The fear of man brings a snare, but whoever leans on, trusts in, and puts his confidence in the Lord is safe and set on high.—Proverbs 29:25 (AMP)

Many people in Saul's army were more experienced and more skilled in warfare than David, but none of them stepped out to face the enemy. Why not?

And what led David to step out and face the enemy with full confidence that he would be victorious, even though he was not a soldier in the army and had no armor to protect him?

David had the confidence of success.

He had already experienced other battles with a lion and with a bear and had been victorious (1 Samuel 17:37). As a result of these successful, victorious experiences, he had a different mind-set than everyone else in Saul's army.

While every soldier in the army had fear in his heart and expected only certain defeat if he ventured out to face the enemy, the thought of defeat didn't even enter David's mind. Because his previous experience in battle had been successful, it never occurred to him that he might lose, so he did not experience the same fear as the soldiers who were much better equipped and trained.

This principle is important to understand. David was the *least qualified* of all those on the battlefield! But what set him apart from the others was a history of successful experiences in similar situations. Having a history of successful, victorious experiences freed him from any fear that the outcome of this new challenge might be anything other than victorious and successful.

We must not give up after one or two discouraging ministry experiences. That is an inseparable part of learning and growing in our gifts and callings.

A good leader will do everything possible to ensure that your ministry experiences are successful and encouraging.

The risk factor should be very gradually increased from *no risk* at first to adventurous, high risk, when God is in it.

When David went out to face Goliath, the fate of the nation of Israel was on the line. The risk factor was very high. But God didn't send David out to face Goliath until He had prepared him for that moment through preliminary fights in which David was only defending sheep. In David's first two fights, the risk factor was much lower. There wasn't nearly as much on the line in his first two fights. When he experienced success in his first two fights, David had the confidence he needed to succeed in a situation where everything was on the line.

Preparation Piece 5: Availability

In order for God to use you in ministry, you must put yourself into a situation where ministry can occur. You must make the first move.

Peter was the only disciple who walked on the water, but he never would have experienced that if he hadn't stepped out of the boat. What about the other disciples who were in the boat with Peter? Could they have walked on water as well? Was the invitation open to them, too?

For there is no partiality with God.—Romans 2:11 (NASB)

If they had desired it enough, wouldn't Jesus have bid them to come as well?

"And I say unto you, Ask, and it shall be given you."—Luke 11:9a (KJV)

But they didn't ask. They didn't put themselves into position to experience the miracle.

It is the same way in ministry. If you want to be used by God in ministry, *you* must desire it. *You* must get off the couch. *You* must place yourself in a position to be used in ministry.

Remarkable things begin to happen when people simply step out and place themselves in positions where ministry can happen! I have seen this more than once. People who have *never* received words of knowledge from the Holy Spirit for another person begin to receive clear revelation *after* they venture outside the walls of the church with a small team to seek out people to whom they can minister.

Joe and his wife attended a prophetic evangelism workshop that I had organized at our church in the Dallas, Texas, area. On the last day of the workshop, we all went out to a train station in Dallas. Those who had attended the workshop were divided into teams of two or three and sent out to find people to minister to in the power of the Spirit.

Joe had accompanied his wife to the workshop, but it had not been his intention to actually participate in the outreach.

After several encounters at the train station, we switched people to different teams. We did this to allow more practice with different partners. As people changed partners, Joe's wife ended up on a team with no men.

I asked Joe if he would mind walking along with these ladies because I didn't feel comfortable sending two ladies out on the streets of Dallas by themselves. Being the gentleman that he is, Joe agreed.

Then a funny thing happened. As Joe accompanied the ladies when they approached people on the street, he began to receive revelation from the Lord about the people they approached! It was undeniable! He began to receive revelation from the Holy Spirit for people they encountered only *after* he took a place on a team at the train station. Before that, when he had stayed on the sidelines, even though he was interceding for the outreach, he received no revelation.

Start with Your Neighbor

Where do we start? Jesus described our neighbor in Luke 10 as anyone who crosses our path who has needs. After relating the story of the Good Samaritan, He commanded us to "Go and do thou likewise."

We don't have to be concerned about launching out to a dark, foreign country to minister. As we are faithful to meet the needs of those who cross our paths, God will expand our ministry—possibly into dark places, but only as we are ready for it. God is trustworthy. We can trust Him not to throw us to the wolves, unprepared and unprotected, so that we end up in a position of danger like the sons of Sceva.

Self-Evaluation:
How Prepared Are You Now?

Objective: To gauge your current level of preparedness. This is not meant to intimidate or discourage you. We all have plenty of room for growth! This self-evaluation will help you realize what kinds of help you can offer to people now and in what areas you have room for growth and improvement in order to be more fully prepared to do the works of Jesus.

1. Equipping

   a. Have you received the Baptism in the Holy Spirit? (Acts 19:2–6)

   b. Have church leaders laid hands on you for the impartation of gifts of the Spirit? (1 Corinthians 12 and 14)

c. Do you take advantage of opportunities to receive spiritual impartations from godly leaders when those opportunities are offered? (1 Timothy 4:14 and 2 Timothy 1:6)

2. Training

   a. Do you search the Word of God for answers to problems?

   b. Do you use tools like concordances, dictionaries, and related software in your study of the Bible?

   c. Are you able to hear God's voice in a variety of ways?

   d. Do you have mentors or teachers you respect and learn from regularly? (Proverbs 13:20)

   e. Do you function in the gifts of the Holy Spirit—prophecy, tongues, interpretation of tongues, words of knowledge, words of wisdom, discernment, healings, miracles, faith—inside and outside of church meetings?

   f. Do you minister physical, mental, and emotional healing to people—inside and outside of church meetings?

   g. Do you help people achieve deliverance from dark spiritual influences—inside and outside of church meetings?

   h. Do you interpret your own dreams and the dreams of others?

   i. Do you know how to baptize someone in water? (Matthew 28:19)

j. Do you know how to lead a believer into the Baptism of the Holy Spirit?

k. Can you clearly explain what someone must do to be saved?

l. Are you able to provide wise counsel to people who have problems in areas such as relationships, character, health, work or school situations, finances, or issues in their relationship with God?

We all have plenty of room for growth in this area! Don't be discouraged! Realize that God will use your own problems to train you to be able to help others who have similar problems.

> First take the log out of your own eye, and then you will see clearly to take the speck out of your brother's eye.— Matthew 7:5 (NASB)

3. Practice

a. Do you have daily scheduled times you set aside for the Word of God and prayer?

b. Do you ask God to speak to you in a variety of ways and keep a journal of what He says to you?

c. Do you read articles and books by wise, godly leaders? Do you watch their videos and listen to their audio messages?

d. Do you take advantage of opportunities to minister to people in church meetings?

e. Do you pray for and minister to the needs of your family members?

f. Do you participate in outreach events?

g. Do you participate in mission trips?

h. Are you alert for "God's appointments" to minister to people that cross your path every day?

4. Confidence

a. In which areas of ministry do you feel *most* confident? These may be areas in which you can provide leadership or guidance for other believers.

b. In which areas of ministry do you feel *least* confident? You may want to focus on getting more training and practice in these areas.

5. Availability

a. How quickly could you rearrange your schedule in order to

• seek God?

• learn or practice skills for ministry?

• minister to someone with desperate needs?

CHAPTER 7
THE MINISTRY MODEL

Our Ultimate Model

> But you have not so learned Christ, if indeed you have heard Him and have been taught by Him, as the truth is in Jesus.—Ephesians 4:20–21 (NKJV)

Very simply, Jesus is our ultimate model for ministry. In fact, one of the very first commands Jesus gave was "*Follow me*, and I will make you fishers of men" in Matthew 4:19 (ESV).

His ministry model was continued in the ministry of the disciples as detailed in the book of Acts and in the epistles. As the Apostle Paul said, "*Follow my example, as I follow the example of Christ.*" (1 Corinthians 11:1 NIV)

We must strive to understand the *ways* of God, not just His acts.

> He made known His *ways* to Moses, His *acts* to the children of Israel.—Psalm 103:7 (NKJV)

We must understand *how* God works, not just *what* He does, so that we can fully cooperate with Him.

The Ministry Focus:
Meet People at Their Point of Need

Jesus' first recorded words after returning from His temptation in the wilderness may be seen as a defining statement for the focus of His ministry.

> Again the next day John was standing with two of his disciples, And he looked at Jesus as He walked along, and said, Look! There is the Lamb of God! The two disciples heard him say this, and they followed Him. But Jesus turned, and as He saw them following Him, He said to them, *What are you looking for? [And what is it you wish?]*—John 1:35–40 (AMP)

At first glance, it is difficult to find patterns in Jesus' ministry encounters with people. It seems as if every encounter was different and unique, with no convenient formulas that would be easy for us to follow, but there is one thing that all of Jesus' ministry encounters had in common. *Jesus always met people at their point of need.*

He made every encounter personally relevant to them, addressing the needs and desires they each had at that particular time in their lives.

Many evangelistic approaches encourage us to steer every encounter toward salvation, but salvation may not be what *that person sees* as his most pressing need. It's more difficult to convince someone of his need for salvation if he's not sure where his next meal is coming from, for instance.

If we continue to force the salvation issue, and even lead the person in a "sinner's prayer," after we leave, the person's focus returns to his most pressing need, and the relationship with

Jesus is tossed aside and thrown out of his life, just as you would toss useless clutter out of your house.

> Suppose a brother or sister has no clothes or food. Suppose one of you says to them, 'Go. I hope everything turns out fine for you. Keep warm. Eat well.' And you do nothing about what they really need. *Then what good have you done?*—James 2:15–16 (NIRV)

As I think back on situations at my workplace when I was able to lead people into a salvation experience, each salvation occurred because the individuals expressed genuine needs, and I was able to connect them with what God had already provided to meet those needs.

When one person was lonely and feeling betrayed by her friends, I told her that Jesus is a friend who "sticks closer than a brother," whose love never wavers for us.

When others felt unsafe and needed assurance of protection, I described the protection that God offers us as our Shield, our Fortress, our Deliverer.

When another individual expressed a need for stability and security, I described Jesus, who promises never to leave or forsake us.

As I think back about the fifteen people I led to salvation at my workplace, I realize I had not approached any of them with a salvation message. I had not approached them at all! I had simply responded to a genuine need that each one expressed. As I described what Jesus had already provided to meet their particular need, salvation was easy. It came very naturally. There was never a hard-sell salvation message. It wasn't necessary. When people saw that God had real answers to meet their needs, they accepted Him eagerly.

Behavior Signals Needs

Sometimes, needs are obvious. Other needs are more difficult to pinpoint. Often behavior signals a need in someone's life, but it may still be a challenge to link that signal to the correct need.

Inappropriate behavior masks an underlying need. The inappropriate behavior could be a cry for help.

Behavioral experts tell us that when a person engages in behavior that is wrong or inappropriate, whether it is mischief or even criminal, it is because he was seeking to meet some need that he had, and he made a poor choice in how to go about it. (Shah, 2013)

A person's needs drive him to take action to try to meet those needs. If a person does not find Jesus, he may turn to temporary substitutes that don't offer real satisfaction, like entertainment, drugs and alcohol, money, career, comfort food, religion, or immoral relationships.

Focus on the Other Person

Jesus made each encounter about *them* and where they were in life, not about Himself: "What are *you* looking for? [And what is it *you* wish?]." Instead of having His own personal agenda for each encounter, he tailored each encounter to the individual, his or her needs and his or her desires.

> *"What do you want me to do for you?"* Jesus asked him. The blind man said, "Rabbi, I want to be able to see."—Mark 10:51 (NIRV)

In that moment, He became their best friend, taking on their goals as His own, walking alongside them to help them achieve what they most needed and desired.

Let each of you look out not only for his own interests, but also for the interests of others.—Philippians 2:4 (NKJV)

Bear one another's burdens, and so fulfill the law of Christ.—Galatians 6:2 (NKJV)

Have No Agenda

In the same way, we must be careful not to have a predetermined agenda of our own for our encounters with people.

In the Church, we've done city-wide outreach backward. We've had our method of outreach, and we've tried to impose it on the city, as if whatever we offered should fit its situation, requiring the city to conform to what we offered instead of finding out what the needs were and then designing our outreach to meet those needs.

A better model would be this:

1. Build relationships.

2. Find out what people need, what would benefit them.

3. *Then* design the outreach to fit that need.

Two basic motivations can guide us in our dealings with people: we can either love them or use them. People have an innate ability to detect which motivation is guiding us.

If we come into an encounter with an agenda, trying to steer a person in a particular direction, like a salesman trying to "close the deal," people will sense that we do not really love them.

They will sense that we are just using them for our own purposes, and they will resist, putting up a wall of protection against our selfish agenda. They will back off and retreat, fortifying their defenses and possibly retaliating, like an army defending itself against an unwelcome force invading its territory.

With Unselfish Love

Jesus' approach was different. He had no selfish motivation. He had no selfish agenda. The Apostle Paul echoed Jesus' selfless motivation:

> And I will very gladly spend and be spent for your souls; *though the more abundantly I love you, the less I am loved.* But be that as it may, I did not burden you.... Did I take advantage of you by any of those whom I sent to you? I urged Titus, and sent our brother with him. Did Titus take advantage of you? Did we not walk in the same spirit? Did we not walk in the same steps? ...But *we do all things, beloved, for your edification.*—2 Corinthians 12:15–19 (NKJV)

People sensed that Jesus had no other motivation but a pure, unselfish love for them and a willingness to meet their deepest needs and desires; and they responded by opening up to Him and crying out to Him to meet the needs they had. The love He expressed was so attractive to them that they followed Him by the hundreds and thousands wherever He went.

Drawing People to Jesus

Jesus makes it clear in John 6:26 that it is *not* demonstrations of the miraculous that cause people to become disciples. People are searching for something that will meet their needs.

Jesus answered them, I assure you, most solemnly I tell you, you have been searching for Me, not because you saw the miracles and signs but *because you were fed with the loaves and were filled and satisfied.*—John 6:26 (AMP)

Too often, our outreach approaches have been focused only on leading people to salvation, ignoring, at least temporarily, any other needs they might have had, no matter how pressing. "After all," we reasoned, "there is no need greater than eternal salvation."

What we have not understood is that when people's needs are truly met, they will naturally be drawn to the source that provided the answers to meet those needs in their lives.

We will experience the greatest effectiveness in our ministry efforts when we purposefully reach out, in the love and power of Jesus Christ, *to meet the needs of the people* we encounter in our daily lives.

God's Priorities for Ministry

If you were raised in an evangelical church, you may have been taught that when you stand before the Lord, you will have to give account for each situation in which you did not share the gospel with someone when you had the opportunity to do so, but Jesus tells us very clearly what He will hold us accountable for in Matthew 25:34–40. Notice what He emphasizes in His criteria:

Then the King will say to those at His right hand, Come, you blessed of My Father [you favored of God and appointed to eternal salvation], inherit (receive as your own) the kingdom prepared for you from the foundation of the world.

For I was hungry and you gave Me food, I was thirsty and you gave Me something to drink, I was a stranger and you brought Me together with yourselves and welcomed and entertained and lodged Me,

I was naked and you clothed Me, I was sick and you visited Me with help and ministering care, I was in prison and you came to see Me.

Then the just and upright will answer Him, Lord, when did we see You hungry and gave You food, or thirsty and gave You something to drink?

And when did we see You a stranger and welcomed and entertained You, or naked and clothed You?

And when did we see You sick or in prison and came to visit You?

And the King will reply to them, Truly I tell you, in so far as you did it for one of the least [in the estimation of men] of these My brethren, you did it for Me.—Matthew 25:34–40 (AMP)

Nowhere in this passage is "witnessing" (sharing the gospel of salvation) even mentioned as a criterion. Of course, we are certainly not saying that we should neglect the preaching of the gospel, but if we preach the gospel without demonstrating the love and power of Jesus to meet the needs of people, we are presenting an incomplete gospel.

In Bob Jones' death experience in August of 1975, he watched as the Lord Jesus Himself stood as The Door to meet people who had just died. Jesus met people one by one and asked them only one question. He did not ask them how many people they witnessed to. He did not ask them how much money they gave to the church. He did not ask them if they were faithful to attend church services. He asked them only this question: "Did you learn to love?" (Jones & Warner).

You can hear Bob Jones tell this story in his own words online. There are several videos on YouTube in which Bob relates this experience himself. Just search for "Bob Jones death experience" or "Bob Jones Did you learn to love?"

Nicodemus

The need for salvation is the most important need in every person's life. Jesus, however, *who knew this better than anyone*, rarely, or actually *never*, began a conversation by talking about a person's need for salvation. You may want to say, "Now, wait a minute! What about Nicodemus in John 3? Jesus started that conversation by saying, 'Truly, truly, I say unto you, Except a man be born again, he cannot see the kingdom of God.'"

That is true. Jesus did begin that conversation by speaking of the necessity of being born again, but that was a theological discussion with a high-ranking Jewish teacher. Jesus' purpose in that conversation seemed to be to expand Nicodemus' understanding of truth, which Nicodemus could then pass along to those within his sphere of influence.

If instead it was an effort to lead Nicodemus to personal salvation; it seems to have been a failure. At the end of the encounter, the two men seem to have gone their separate ways. There is no record that Nicodemus followed Jesus as one of His disciples after that encounter. In John 7:50, Nicodemus was back with the Pharisees, "being one of them." There is no evidence that Nicodemus was converted or ever confessed Jesus as Messiah, although he was sympathetic to Jesus' cause and, with Joseph of Arimathaea, cared for Jesus' body after His death.

Usually in outreach ministry, the Church has had an agenda that was pushed—pushing people toward salvation. In contrast, Jesus flipped that completely around and asked, "What do *you* want? What do *you* need? What is it *you* are seeking? What are *your* goals?" Our focus must be the same.

At this point, I would highly recommend that you put this book down and read chapter 10 of "Angels on Assignment" by Roland Buck (Buck, Hunter, & Hunter). You can read the entire book online at www.angelsonassignment.org, or you can order a paper copy from Amazon.com or many other online book sellers.

Roland Buck was a pastor in Boise, Idaho, who had the remarkable experience of being visited by angels of God many times. As wonderful as his angelic visitations were, the message they brought from the heart of God is much, much more valuable. I highly recommend reading the entire book, but for now, please take time to read chapter 10, "When God Says Thanks!"

Discipleship Practice:
Seeing the Needs Around Us

Objective: To become more alert to the needs of people around us and begin preparing to meet those needs.

1. List a few of the people with whom you communicate on a regular basis.

2. Beside each person's name, list at least one of his or her most pressing needs.

   a. If you are unaware of someone's needs, take that as a signal that you need to take time to ask appropriate questions, listen, and learn more about what he or she is going through at this time in his or her life.

3. Choose one person's need, and commit to helping him or her meet that need. In doing this, you will be fulfilling Christ's command:

This is My commandment, that you love one another as I have loved you. Greater love has no one than this, than to lay down one's life for his friends.—John 15: 12–13 (NKJV)

You may need to gain more knowledge or skills in order to meet the person's need. Realize that if you prepare yourself to minister effectively to *one* person's need, you will also be prepared to help *many others* who have similar needs. This growth experience will give you more "tools" for your "tool belt."

CHAPTER 8
FOCUS ON NEEDS

Where God's Interests Are

As the angel told Roland Buck, if we want to see what God's interests really are, we can find them in the fifty-eighth chapter of Isaiah:

> [Rather] is not this the fast that I have chosen: to loose the bonds of wickedness, to undo the bands of the yoke, to let the oppressed go free, and that you break every [enslaving] yoke?
>
> Is it not to divide your bread with the hungry and bring the homeless poor into your house—when you see the naked, that you cover him, and that you hide not yourself from [the needs of] your own flesh and blood?
>
> Then shall your light break forth like the morning, and your healing (your restoration and the power of a new life) shall spring forth speedily; your righteousness (your rightness, your justice, and your right relationship with God) shall go

before you [conducting you to peace and prosperity], and the glory of the Lord shall be your rear guard.

Then you shall call, and the Lord will answer; you shall cry, and He will say, Here I am. If you take away from your midst yokes of oppression [wherever you find them], the finger pointed in scorn [toward the oppressed or the godly], and every form of false, harsh, unjust, and wicked speaking,

And if you pour out that with which you sustain your own life for the hungry and satisfy the need of the afflicted, then shall your light rise in darkness, and your obscurity and gloom become like the noonday.

And the Lord shall guide you continually and satisfy you in drought and in dry places and make strong your bones. And you shall be like a watered garden and like a spring of water whose waters fail not.

And your ancient ruins shall be rebuilt; you shall raise up the foundations of [buildings that have laid waste for] many generations; and you shall be called Repairer of the Breach, Restorer of Streets to Dwell In.—Isaiah 58:6–12 (AMP)

Meet People at Their Point of Need

So many things we focus on in life—and in ministry—have little or no lasting value. People do. People matter. People have lasting value—so much so that Jesus was willing to pay the ultimate price for them.

When we focus on meeting the needs of people, *then* we have a life and a ministry that God honors and rewards.

Suppose a brother or sister has no clothes or food. Suppose one of you says to them, 'Go. I hope everything turns out fine for you. Keep warm. Eat well.' And you do nothing about what they really need. Then what good have you done?—James 2:15–16 (NIRV)

God considered Job to be a "perfect man" (Job 1:8). This is how Job described his own life and ministry:

All who heard me praised me. All who saw me spoke well of me. For I assisted the poor in their need and the orphans who required help. I helped those without hope, and they blessed me. And I caused the widows' hearts to sing for joy. Everything I did was honest. Righteousness covered me like a robe, and I wore justice like a turban. I served as eyes for the blind and feet for the lame. I was a father to the poor and assisted strangers who needed help. I broke the jaws of godless oppressors and plucked their victims from their teeth.—Job 29:11–17 (NLT)

When Jesus began His ministry, he declared His own "mission statement":

The Spirit of the LORD is upon Me, Because He has anointed Me To preach the gospel to the poor; He has sent Me to heal the brokenhearted, To proclaim liberty to the captives And recovery of sight to the blind, To set at liberty those who are oppressed; To proclaim the acceptable year of the LORD.—Luke 4:18–19 (NKJV)

There is one thing that all of Jesus' ministry encounters had in common. *Jesus always met people at their point of need.* As he said to Andrew,

"What are you looking for? [And what is it you wish?]"—
John 1:35–40 (AMP)

The Example of Heidi and Rolland Baker

Heidi and Rolland Baker of Iris Ministries have adopted this focus of meeting the needs of individuals they encounter, and they demonstrate this in many ways. They constantly reinforce this focus by saying things like "stop for the one," "love the one," and "just love the one in front of you" (Velu, 2004).

At this point, stop reading. Find the film "Mama Heidi," and watch it! You can buy or rent the DVD from Amazon.com and many other Christian and secular retail sellers. You may also be able watch it online via Netflix, Amazon Prime, or other streaming video services.

Heidi and Rolland Baker are the best living examples of people "doing the works of Jesus" that I know of. The film, "Mama Heidi," takes you into their lives and their ministry. It shows their focus on meeting the needs of those they encounter. They get it right. They do not minister with a predetermined agenda. They go to where the people are, discover their needs, and then do what they can to meet those needs. Sometimes the needs are spiritual, however most of their time seems to be spent meeting physical and emotional needs. They provide solutions for needs in the areas of health, education, food and water, shelter, family, clothing, as well as sharing the good news of salvation through Christ. They provide love—in whatever form it is needed.

As you watch the film, you'll see many expressions of genuine love demonstrated:

- Five hundred people have been taken in to live with them; eight boys live with them in their own home.

- They went out into a very risky situation, trusting God, not putting their own needs first.

- They went to the unlovely, the outcasts, the ones who could not care for themselves.

- They *search out* people who have needs, not waiting for people to come to them.

- They invest personal time with individuals daily.

- They treat each person as a valuable individual. They are alert to individual needs. When new people come to live with them, they take showers in the Bakers' own home.

- They take time to get to know each person and learn details about their lives.

- They see potential in each person.

- They demonstrate God's love *first* and explain the gospel later.

- The staff is "overstretched" because the need is so great.

- As they have been faithful to focus on meeting the needs of the individual, God has honored them and expanded their influence worldwide.

- They started in a building that nobody wanted—"the worst of the worst."

- They endure despite hardships, thefts, exhaustion, persecution, and government interference.

- Heidi is called "Mama" and is seen as a mother figure, even by people who are not involved in her ministry.

- They believe Jesus' promise to them: "I died so that there would always be enough." So they never turn away a child who has needs.

- They minister to "the whole person"—meeting whatever needs each person has.

- They go where other ministers will not go. They said "yes" when other ministers said "no" to the calling.

- There is an abundance of fruit from the ministry as those who have been rescued begin to rescue others.

- They seek what is best for the people they serve.

- They trust God daily for their basic needs.

- Their joy is in seeing others succeed after being rescued from the streets.

- Where would those people be if Heidi and Rolland had not gone to them?

   As Heidi and Rolland say in the film,

- "Our life has been a continuous story of giving away."

- "Just love the one in front of you."

- "If you say you love God, then you will love the person in front of you."

- "Changing people one by one will change whole nations."

Then the King will say to those on his right, "Come, you who are blessed by my Father; take your inheritance, the kingdom prepared for you since the creation of the world. For I was hungry and you gave me something to eat, I was thirsty and you gave me something to drink, I was a stranger and you invited me in, I needed clothes and you clothed me, I was sick and you looked after me, I was in prison and you came to visit me."

Then the righteous will answer him, "Lord, when did we see you hungry and feed you, or thirsty and give you something to drink? When did we see you a stranger and invite you in, or needing clothes and clothe you? When did we see you sick or in prison and go to visit you?"

The King will reply, "I tell you the truth, whatever you did for one of the least of these brothers of mine, you did for me."—Matthew 25:34–40 (NIV)

CHAPTER 9
BE A DOER, NOT JUST A HEARER

But be doers of the word, and not hearers only, deceiving yourselves.—James 1:22 (ESV)

Suppose a brother or sister has no clothes or food. Suppose one of you says to them, 'Go. I hope everything turns out fine for you. Keep warm. Eat well.' And you do nothing about what they really need. *Then what good have you done?*—James 2:15–16 (NIRV)

But as for me, when they were sick, my clothing was sackcloth; I afflicted myself with fasting, and I prayed with head bowed on my breast. I behaved as if grieving for my friend or my brother; I bowed down in sorrow, as one who bewails his mother.—Psalm 35:13–14 (AMP)

Discipleship Practice:
Turn Your Prayer List into a Needs List

Objectives: To help us become more aware of the needs of others and to focus on meeting those needs.

Too often, when we put people on our "prayer list," we limit ourselves *only* to praying for them. If we turn our prayer list into a "needs list," we may be more likely to get involved in meeting the needs in people's lives.

- Make it your goal not to put anyone on your prayer list unless you are willing to personally get involved in helping to meet that person's needs, when it is possible and appropriate.

- When you agree to put someone on your prayer list, consider it a personal commitment to walk with that person through that situation until the prayer is answered. This may not always be possible or practical, but if we have this as our goal, we will be much closer to "bearing one another's burdens, and so fulfilling the law of Christ" (Galatians 6:2).

- When we are willing to get involved in helping to meet the needs of those we pray for, we will begin to develop genuine love for them as a result:

  For where your treasure is, there will your heart be also.— Luke 12:34 (AMP)

Discipleship Practice:
Include Others in Your Prayers for Yourself

Objectives: To help us develop hearts of servants, expressing genuine love for others by praying for their needs as if they were our own.

As you pray for yourself, asking God to bless *you* in different ways, think of other people in your life who could benefit from the same blessings. Pray that God would bless *them* in the same ways that you are asking God to bless *you*. Include them in your prayers when you are praying for yourself.

(Praying for God to bless *your enemies* can be a great way to help you conquer any bitterness toward them!)

For example, to do this using the Lord's Prayer, you might pray something like this:

"Our Father in heaven, hallowed be Your name. Your kingdom come. Your will be done on earth as it is in heaven. *For myself, my family and especially for Eric and Stacy, who have really been struggling lately*, give us this day our daily bread..."

Do not merely look out for your own personal interests, but also for the interests of others.—Philippians 2:4 (NASB)

You shall love your neighbor *as yourself*.—Mark 12:31 (AMP)

And the LORD restored Job's losses *when he prayed for his friends*. Indeed the LORD gave Job twice as much as he had before."—Job 42:10 (NKJV)

"Therefore, confess your sins to one another and *pray for one another, that you may be healed.*"—James 5:16 (ESV)

Feed the Relationship

Opportunities for ministry often arise within the context of relationships. A person rarely ever reveals deep, personal problems to a stranger.

It may be years before a friend feels comfortable enough to confide in you about some of his or her deepest needs. For this reason, it is vital to stay open to the relationship. Nurture and strengthen the relationship. He or she may even try to push you away, but in some cases, you may need to adopt the posture of Ruth when Naomi tried to get rid of her:

May the Lord punish me severely if I allow anything but death to separate us! - Ruth 1:17b (NLT)

This doesn't mean that you turn people into projects. You'll be most effective if you have no agenda but relationship. Just be there! If people believe that you will always be there for them if they need something, they will be much more inclined to share their real problems with you. Then you will be positioned to share God's answers with them when the time is right.

Go the Extra Mile

Go the extra mile. Intentionally look for ways to *go beyond what is expected* in showing love to people. Send a note. Send a card on a day other than a birthday. Spend time with them. Make yourself available for them. Give them a call. Point out qualities that you admire about them. Buy a book for them, and write encouraging words to them inside the cover. Send them flowers. Tell them when you are thinking of them and praying for them. Remind them of good memories you have of them.

Set Your Boundaries

Sometimes, when you get more involved in the lives of those around you, they may try to take advantage of your kindness. There may be situations in which you feel you are being used by people to further their own personal agendas. If these situations threaten to prevent you from fulfilling your responsibilities to God, yourself, or others, you may have to set firm boundaries to protect yourself from inappropriate attempts to use or abuse you. If people do not place appropriate boundaries on themselves in their dealings with you, then you may need to set boundaries for them.

For example, one of my favorite places to minister to people is at a train station. But when other believers come with me, I advise them not to bring any money with them. Then when someone at the train station asks for a handout, it will be easier to redirect the conversation to the person's real needs. Peter demonstrated this with the man at the Beautiful gate of the temple:

> But Peter said, "I have no silver or gold, but what I have I give you; in the name of Jesus Christ of Nazareth, stand up and walk." - Acts 3:6 (NRSV)

Giving the man money would have insured that his situation would not change. Healing him from his crippled condition met his real need and changed his life forever.

Jesus had to constantly protect Himself and His ministry from those who would steer it off-track, intentionally or unintentionally:

But Jesus did not commit Himself to them, because He knew all men, and had no need that anyone should testify of man, for He knew what was in man.—John 2:24–25 (NKJV)

Nehemiah also was quick to discern and reject attempts to distract him from the real purpose of his life:

So I sent messengers to them, saying, "I am doing a great work and I cannot come down. Why should the work stop while I leave it to come down to you?"—Nehemiah 6:3 (NRSV)

Not Open to Jesus

Many people are not open to even talk about Jesus. They may be atheists, agnostics, or they may hold different religious beliefs. There may be many reasons they are not open.

In these cases, it typically does no good to force the issues of Jesus, the Bible, or salvation on people with this mind-set. Most likely, the Father is not drawing them yet.

"No one is able to come to Me [Jesus] unless the Father Who sent Me attracts and draws him and gives him the desire to come to Me..." (John 6:44 AMP)

The best approach here, rather than forcing conversations about Jesus, may be to cooperate with God by praying that the Father would draw them to Jesus. Nurture the relationships with them. Be there for them. As you pray, God may allow problems or needs to come into their lives. These problems or needs may be the very things that motivate them to look beyond themselves for help. When these friends, acquaintances, or family members come to you for help with their problems, then you may have opportunities to share God's solutions to meet their needs.

If you don't have the answers to their problems, don't dismiss them. God has the answers. Ask Him. Then be alert to recognize the answers when they come.

"Ask, and it will be given you; search, and you will find; knock, and the door will be opened for you. For everyone who asks receives, and everyone who searches finds, and for everyone who knocks, the door will be opened." - Matthew 7:7-8 (NRSV)

Skeptical but Open

Some people are skeptical about Jesus, but they may express some curiosity or interest in knowing more about Him. In these situations, it may be best to answer their questions fully, explaining things as clearly as you can in a very straightforward manner without trying to "push them" in any particular direction.

If you don't have all the answers to their questions, admit it honestly. Tough questions may be asked to test you. Will you make something up, playing the part of a know-it-all, or will you honestly admit that you don't have all the answers? Skeptics aren't looking for a know-it-all. They're looking for a genuinely honest Christian—someone who lives the faith he professes.

The person asking you questions is trying to gather information in order to make a decision that will have eternal consequences for him or her. Be honest. Be straightforward. Be real.

But also be careful. Don't do anything to damage the relationship if possible. Do not offend needlessly. Do *not* push! Do not expect an instant decision from him or her.

Jesus allowed Peter and the other disciples to follow Him for months before He finally asked them what they thought of Him (See Matthew 16:13-17). Don't the people you encounter deserve the same consideration? After all, the decision to follow Christ is a lot more important than choosing a college or choosing a career, and *those* decisions can take *years* for some people!

Expanding Your Influence

As you are faithful to learn how to respond appropriately to the individuals who cross your path, God will expand your influence to other groups of people: other Christian denominations, other religions, Muslims, Buddhists, Hindus, New Agers, Occultists, atheists, and even your family members.

That's been my experience.

CHAPTER 10
WILL YOU ACCEPT THE CALL?

Where Do We Go From Here?

We have been focusing on basic principles that guided Jesus' ministry and that should guide our own lives and ministries as well:

- Most significant ministry opportunities happen outside of church meetings.

- Many divine appointments come our way as interruptions, in between scheduled events, as we go about our daily business.

- Focus on the needs of individuals who cross our paths.

We've highlighted an example in Heidi Baker of someone who is actually Doing the Works of Jesus and is living the life of a Disciple Who Loves.

This is just the beginning!

Church leadership must be committed to providing support to help us prepare to minister in the same ways.

- Equipping

- Training

- Practice

But even if church leaders don't provide all of the support we need, God can provide these things if we ask Him. He can become your personal mentor and trainer, as He was for Samuel, Moses, David, Elijah, and so many others!

Do not wait for leaders; do it alone, person to person.— Mother Teresa

The next step is to prepare, and then move into God's high calling as individuals and as a church—developing skills and confidence—and making ourselves available for ministry.

Will You Accept God's High Calling?

Now that you see what God is asking for, His question to you is "Will you accept the Call?"

You are at a crossroads. You can either accept the higher calling that God is offering you or you can go on with business as usual.

The verse that you need to be aware of in this hour is 2 Chronicles 16:9:

For the eyes of the LORD run to and fro throughout the whole earth, to give strong support to those whose heart is blameless toward him.—2 Chronicles 16:9 (ESV)

The Lord is searching the whole earth to find *someone* who will accept His high calling. If you accept His high calling, the Lord is standing by to strongly support you in it. If you decide to go on with business as usual, the eyes of the Lord will move on to look for someone else, and He will take this offer to them.

How do I know that? Because Scripture gives witness that this is God's way. In Scripture, the Lord gave us stories of individuals and groups of people who rejected His high calling, and decided to go their own way instead.

When the children of Israel rejected God's high calling and instead demanded to have a king and be like all the other nations, God told Samuel, "Obey the voice of the people in all that they say to you, for they have not rejected you, but they have rejected me from being king over them."—1 Samuel 8:7 (ESV)

Then later, God had to leave King Saul and move His anointing on to David.

Now the Spirit of the LORD departed from Saul...—1 Samuel 16:14 (ESV)

Jesus warned the church of Ephesus that they were in danger of losing their place in God's perfect plan if they did not change their ways and return to what they knew was best:

Nevertheless I have this against you, that you have left your first love. Remember therefore from where you have fallen; repent and do the first works, or else I will come to you quickly and remove your lampstand from its place—unless you repent.—Revelation 2:4–5 (NKJV)

The Apostle Paul fully realized that his place in the plan of God was assured only as long as He continued to walk in obedience and submission to God: "But I discipline my body and keep it under control, lest after preaching to others I myself should be disqualified."—1 Corinthians 9:27 (ESV)

What we've got to realize is that God's plan is much bigger than we are. He is offering us an opportunity to be a part of His overall plan of the ages. We can accept His offer or reject it, but if we reject it, He will move on because His plan must be accomplished.

Let's look at the bigger picture of what God is moving toward in church history, and where we fit into His plan.

The Restoration of All Things

Jesus' life was the ultimate demonstration of God's love and power in ministry, but after His ascension, the Church slowly began to lose touch with that. Finally, the Church lost sight of almost everything that Jesus' ministry represented and slipped into the Dark Ages, in which even the Word of God itself was withheld from the people, and it was spoken only in Latin, and only the church leaders were allowed to read it!

Then God began to restore what the Church had lost since the time of Jesus' ministry. Luther restored the doctrine of justification by faith, and the Bible was printed and distributed in the common language of the people.

Over the years, God has worked to restore other key concepts and doctrines—Repentance, Baptism, Healing, and Gifts of the Spirit.

As the Church experienced this slow process of restoration of all things that had been lost since Jesus' time, the predominant message of the Church changed, over the course of the centuries, to match what God was restoring at that time.

For a while, many preachers were focusing on "hellfire and brimstone" messages, like Charles Finney and Jonathan Edwards. Jonathan Edwards' most famous sermon was entitled "Sinners in the Hands of an Angry God." At that time, these messages were exactly what was needed, but those same messages will not get the same reaction today. Today those same messages are likely to turn people off, and maybe even turn people *away* from God. Why?

God has moved on. It's not that those messages are any less true now than they were then. It's just that the predominant need is different now.

God announced a new phase in the restoration of all things when He sent Gabriel with a message to Roland Buck in 1977 (Buck, Hunter, & Hunter). It's interesting that William Branham spoke of the significance of 1977 way back in 1933 when he said that something would happen in 1977 that would transition the church from the "Church" age into the "Kingdom" age (Branham). This message is in line with the heart of what I've been trying to convey in this book. This is also in agreement with the message and example of Heidi and Rolland Baker. Finally, this is also in agreement with Bob Jones' death experience when he witnessed Jesus asking people only one question before they were allowed to enter into their eternal reward: "Did you learn to love?" These messages all agree.

And finally, this is also the message of Scripture, especially in the words of Matthew 25:31–46 and in the example of Jesus' life and ministry.

Just Start. Just Go.

We may think that we are unqualified in some way to enter into this high calling. God doesn't care about that. He prefers it that way. It is almost impossible for God to use a bunch of know-it-alls.

When God called Abraham, He just told Him to go. It wasn't important for Abraham to know all of the details about the journey when he started out.

By faith Abraham obeyed when he was called to go out to a place that he was to receive as an inheritance. And he went out, *not knowing where he was going.*—Hebrews 11:8 (ESV)

God is presenting His Calling to us in this hour. How we respond will determine whether He stays here with us and uses us to fulfill His highest purposes in this hour, or whether He moves on...and presents this offer to someone else.

For many are called, but few are chosen.—Matthew 22:14 (KJV)

Here is what will happen. If we choose to accept this call, on faith of course, like Abraham did, not knowing exactly what it will mean for our future, God will immediately begin to shower His blessings on us, and lead us into the most meaningful, fulfilling lives that we could ever want—better than we could ever imagine.

But as it is written: 'Eye has not seen, nor ear heard, nor have entered into the heart of man the things which God has prepared for those who love Him.—1 Corinthians 2:9 (NKJV)

On the other hand, if we reject this offer, either by saying "no," or by simply doing nothing, God will give us a relatively short grace period in which to change our minds and accept His call, but then He will move on and present this offer to someone else.

Then Jesus told a story. "A man had a fig tree," he said. "It had been planted in his vineyard. When he went to look for fruit on it, he didn't find any. So he went to the man who took care of the vineyard. He said, 'For three years now I've been coming to look for fruit on this fig tree. But I haven't found any. Cut it down! Why should it use up the soil?'

"'Sir,' the man replied, 'leave it alone for one more year. I'll dig around it and feed it. If it bears fruit next year, fine! If not, then cut it down.'"—Luke 13:6–9 (NIRV)

If that happens to our local church and God moves on to another church, we will be reduced to just empty routines, working to keep our church programs and traditions going—but the life will be gone. We'll be reduced to serving empty church programs.

Seeing a lone fig tree by the road, He came to it and found nothing on it except leaves only; and He said to it, "No longer shall there ever be any fruit from you." And at once the fig tree withered.—Matthew 21:19 (NASB)

When Jesus came to evaluate this plant, He found only leaves. He found no fruit. When He found only leaves, He pronounced judgment on the plant and then moved on, away from it. To understand why He reacted this way, we have to understand the purposes of leaves and fruit.

Leaves provide a way for the plant to feed *itself*, through photosynthesis.

Fruit is grown to feed *others*.

Whenever Jesus evaluates a church, if He finds it completely focused inward, feeding itself, His favor will eventually lift, and He will move on to find another church that is reaching out to meet the needs of others. The first church will wither and seem as if it is dead.

Throughout Church history, this has been God's way. Beginning with the Catholic Church in the 1500s, when God came to that "fig tree" to evaluate it, He found it focused inward, enriching itself and neglecting the needs of the people. When the Catholic Church refused to be reformed after the admonitions of Martin Luther and others, God moved on with the Protestant Reformation of the 1500s, leaving the Catholic Church to continue on with its traditions and rituals but empty of the vibrant life of God.

Does God still have genuine believers in the Catholic Church? Of course!

Consider the shining example of Mother Teresa. Her words speak volumes! (Teresa)

> "I try to give to the poor people for love what the rich could get for money. No, I wouldn't touch a leper for a thousand pounds; yet I willingly cure him for the love of God."

> "Many people mistake our work for our vocation. Our vocation is the love of Jesus."

> "Let us not be satisfied with just giving money. Money is not enough. Money can be got, but they need your hearts to love them. So, spread your love everywhere you go."

> "If you want a love message to be heard, it has got to be sent out. To keep a lamp burning, we have to keep putting oil in it."

> "We ourselves feel that what we are doing is just a drop in the ocean. But the ocean would be less because of that missing drop."

> "Intense love does not measure, it just gives."

> "I have found the paradox, that if you love until it hurts, there can be no more hurt, only more love."

"Spread love everywhere you go. Let no one ever come to you without leaving happier."

"Love is a fruit in season at all times, and within reach of every hand."

"Joy is a net of love by which you can catch souls."

"The biggest disease today is not leprosy or tuberculosis, but rather the feeling of being unwanted."

"One of the greatest diseases is to be nobody to anybody."

"Being unwanted, unloved, uncared for, forgotten by everybody, I think that is a much greater hunger, a much greater poverty than the person who has nothing to eat."

"The hunger for love is much more difficult to remove than the hunger for bread."

"Loneliness and the feeling of being unwanted is the most terrible poverty."

"We think sometimes that poverty is only being hungry, naked and homeless. The poverty of being unwanted, unloved and uncared for is the greatest poverty. We must start in our own homes to remedy this kind of poverty."

"I want you to be concerned about your next door neighbor. Do you know your next door neighbor?"

"Love begins at home, and it is not how much we do...but how much love we put in that action."

"Love begins by taking care of the closest ones—the ones at home."

"Let us touch the dying, the poor, the lonely and the unwanted according to the graces we have received and let us not be ashamed or slow to do the humble work."

"Be faithful in small things because it is in them that your strength lies."

"If you can't feed a hundred people, then feed just one."

"Each one of them is Jesus in disguise."

I'm calling for heaven and earth to give witness against you this very day. I'm offering you the choice of life or death. You can choose either blessings or curses. But I want you to choose life. Then you and your children will live.— Deuteronomy 30:19 (NIRV)

I urge you to choose to accept God's high calling!

Move on to aggressively pursue training and preparation.

Seek ministry opportunities that will propel you into the high calling that God has for you!

Book 2: Sowing and Reaping

In Book 2 of this series, "Sowing and Reaping," we will begin to examine each of Jesus' ministry encounters one by one and learn how to really do what Jesus did!

The grace of the Lord Jesus Christ, and the love of God, and the communion of the Holy Spirit be with you all. Amen.—2 Corinthians 13:14 (NKJV)

BIBLIOGRAPHY

Addison, D. (2005). *Prophecy, Dreams, and Evangelism: Revealing God's Love Through Divine Encounters.* (C. Blunk, E. Freeman, D. Kreindler, & M. Ballotte, Eds.) North Sutton, New Hampshire, USA: Streams Publishing House.

Addison, D. (2005). *Prophetic Evangelism Workshop Student Guide.* Santa Monica, California, USA: InLight Connection.

Baker, R., & Baker, H. (2003). *Always Enough: God's Miraculous Provision among the Poorest Children on Earth* (Reprinted ed.). Chosen Books.

Boyle, Gregory (2010-02-14). *Tattoos on the Heart: The Power of Boundless Compassion* (p. 70). Free Press. Kindle Edition.

Branham, W. (2006, July 30). *The Laodicean Church Age.* Retrieved from WilliamBranham.com: http://www.williambranham.com/the_seven_church_ages/the-laodicean-church-age/

Buck, R. H. (Composer). (1979). Sequel to the Throne Room. [R. H. Buck, Performer] On *Sermons from the Man Who Talked With Angels, Vol. 1*. Boise, Idaho, USA.

Buck, R., Hunter, C., & Hunter, F. (n.d.). *Angels on Assignment*. Retrieved from Angels on Assignment: http://angelsonassignment.org/index2.html.

Carnegie, D. (1936). *How to Win Friends and Influence People*. Simon and Schuster.

Davis, P. K. (2011, August 20). *Paul Keith Davis: New Life Rice Lake*. (New Life Christian Church) Retrieved from YouTube: http://www.youtube.com/watch?v=Rw54FBNWryc

Grady, J. L. (n.d.). *Heidi Baker's Uncomfortable Message to America*. Retrieved July 2013, from CBN.com: http://www.cbn.com/spirituallife/churchandministry/C harisma_Grady_HeidiBaker.aspx

Jackson, J. P. (2007, November 16). *Storms, Faith and the Miraculous*. Retrieved from YouTube: https://www.youtube.com/watch?v=WZVwUVNyhJ8

Jones, B., & Warner, S. (n.d.). *Bob Jones' Testimony August 8, 1975 Death Experience*. Retrieved from The Quickened Word: http://www.thequickenedword.com/rhema/BobJonesT estimonyAugust81975DeathExperience.htm

Scott, D., Nimmo, B., & Rabey, S. (2000). *Rachel's Tears: The Spiritual Journey of Columbine Martyr Rachel Scott*. Thomas Nelson Publishers.

Shah, S. (2013, March 31). *Understanding inappropriate behaviour*. Retrieved from Live with loss: http://livewithloss.com/inappropriate/

Stafford, T. (2012, May). Miracles in Mozambique: How Mama Heidi Reaches the Abandoned. *Christianity Today, 56(5)*.

Teresa, M. (n.d.). *Mother Teresa Quotes*. Retrieved from BrainyQuote: http://www.brainyquote.com/quotes/authors/m/mother_teresa.html

Teresa, M. (n.d.). *Mother Teresa Quotes*. Retrieved from Goodreads: https://www.goodreads.com/author/quotes/838305.Mother_Teresa

Teresa, M. (n.d.). *Mother Teresa Quotes*. Retrieved from Catholic Bible 101: http://www.catholicbible101.com/motherteresaquotes.htm

Velu, E. (Producer), Velu, E. (Writer), & Velu, E. (Director). (2004). *Mama Heidi* [Motion Picture].

ABOUT THE AUTHOR

Alan Drake is a career educator with over 25 years' experience in public education. He holds a Bachelor's degree in Elementary Education from Dallas Baptist University and a Master's degree in Educational Administration from East Texas State University.

In addition to his career, Alan has served as a leader in church youth ministry, college and career ministry, outreach ministry, missions and teaching ministry. He has led and participated in organized missions and outreach events in North America and in Europe, in churches, at festivals, on city streets, in restaurants, shopping malls, conferences, workshops, while riding public transportation, and in a wide variety of everyday situations.

Alan is an engaging speaker and teacher. He has taught courses and led workshops, church meetings and conference sessions in North America and in Europe. He currently resides in Dallas, Texas.

FOR MORE INFORMATION

Doing the Works of Jesus
Courses, Conferences and Training

Courses, conferences and training sessions are offered in order to prepare believers to Do the Works of Jesus. These are led and taught by Alan Drake and other ministers experienced and skilled in Doing the Works of Jesus. Alan Drake works with host leaders and ministers to customize and personalize these sessions in order to best meet the needs of the participants within the given time constraints.

Sessions typically include interactive teaching—using a variety of presentation media—, demonstrations, prayers of impartation, practical hands-on activities, and feedback.

These sessions are offered on a limited basis to groups of any size. Scheduling is limited because of Alan Drake's work schedule and other commitments.

Bulk Orders

Bulk prices are available for various quantities of *Doing the Works of Jesus* volumes. For more information, please visit: www.spiritofwisdompublications.com.

Contact the Author

For more information about follow-up classes, practical hands-on training, or scheduling Alan Drake as a speaker, please contact the author:

Alan Drake
c/o Spirit of Wisdom Publications
PO Box 180216
Dallas, TX 75218
Email: alan@spiritofwisdompublications.com
Web: www.spiritofwisdompublications.com
Facebook: www.facebook.com/alandrake